A BATTLE FOR LIVING

The Life and Experiences of Lavina Eastlick

The battle for a living has been a long struggle,
but thus far I am victorious.
Lavina Eastlick

John Isch

ISBN 978-0-9765095-7-8

Picture Credits

Front Cover: Mike Eischen
Brown County Historical Society, New Ulm, MN: Fig. 1
Blue Earth County Historical Society, Mankato, MN: Fig. 2, 3
Bernie Koenigs, Mankato, MN: Fig. 4
Minnesota Historical Society, St. Paul, MN: Figs. 10, 17, 19, 20
Olmsted County History Center, Rochester, MN: Figs. 11, 13, 21
Freeman Family, Andy Birchill, Lougheed, Alberta, Canada: Figs. 15, 18, 22, 24, 25
Gilcrease Museum, Tulsa, OK: Plates 14, 15, 16
All others: Author
Maps: Author

Published by the Brown County Historical Society
1 North Broadway
New Ulm, Minnesota 56073

Table of Contents

Pictures

Plates

ALL PLATES FOLLOW PAGE 95

A Note on Sources

The Eastlicks and the McDonnells were quiet and unassuming folks. They farmed, they married, they raised kids, they lived and died and they only made the newspapers at the latter event, and sometimes not even then. They likely wrote letters and some may even have kept a diary, but they were never famous enough to have someone save their letters and journals and donate them to a prestigious library. They are hard people to write about 100 years after they died. So the teller of their story has to use less interesting artifacts such as census information and land records. The part of this story that tells of their families, where they lived, and when they moved from one place to another is documented in the Federal Censuses of 1860, 1870, 1880, 1900, 1910, 1920, and 1930; from the Minnesota Territorial and State Censuses of 1865, 1875, 1885, 1895, and 1905; from land records in Blue Earth County, Wright County, and Alberta; from the Canadian and Manitoba, Saskatchewan, and Alberta Censuses of 1906, 1911, 1916; from court documents and newspaper articles from Blue Earth County, Hennipin County, and Innisfail (Alberta) showing births, marriages, deaths, and divorces. Lavina and Merton were in the spotlight in 1862 as a result of Merton carrying his brother across the prairie. Lavina, building on that fame that also appeared in the newspapers, wrote her book and added an Appendix in 1900. That provided information to fill out the story, information, of course, from the perspective of Lavina. Some of the histories of Minnesota mentioned the Eastlicks as victims at Shetek. A history of Lougheed, Alberta, contains brief biographies of some of the McDonnells and Freemans. The archival collections at the historical societies of Murray County, Wright County, Olmsted County, Brown County and the Minnesota Historical Society have a number of unpublished documents relating to Shetek. References are provided in the text for published material or manuscripts, but references are not provided for census or land record information, lest the footnotes overwhelm the text. There were a few times when family trees posted on Ancestry.com were consulted, but information was used from these family trees only where there was independent supporting information from published sources. There are a few persons still alive in Canada who knew Laura and through her, Lavina. Andy Birchill owns the land and house where Laura and Angus lived and where Lavina died. Albert Smith, a fellow Seventh Day Adventist, remembers the McDonnells and recalls reading as a child Lavina's book. Jim Wright is a grand nephew of Laura and knows the Freeman family. Interviews, letters, and e-mail with these three, who were generous with their time, filled out some of the bare facts. Descendants of the Pettibones, Eastlicks, and Donald McDonnell were contacted, but no replies were received. On the whole, the documents are few and the hidden secrets, which biographers seem to relish, remain secret. But this paucity of data and information is appropriate. Quiet and unassuming folks have every right to remain so.

Terminology

One hundred fifty years have passed since the events of 1862. Over that time span, the perspective and analysis of the events of that year have changed. Even the words themselves have changed. It was a "massacre" in 1862; today the preferred term is the 1862 US-Dakota War. In 1862 "redskins" or "savages" killed the white settlers. But those terms are, first, racially derogatory and, second, dismissive and characterize a group as inferior. The term that resulted from Columbus's mistake, "Indians," has risen and fallen in favor. "Native American" can describe anyone born in the United States (or, more widely, in America). In point of fact, these words are terms that were applied by those who conquered the indigenous people of the Americas; it was not a name chosen by the people themselves. (First Nation people is the preferred term in Canada, but it is cumbersome and it is also a term coined by those who conquered to describe those who were conquered.)

There appears to be a growing preference by the descendants of the indigenous people to be called by their tribal or national name. That has two advantages. Some of the tribal or national names have a basis in the name the indigenous people called themselves, although the name often went through various translations and misinterpretations from the early European explorers. Second, and probably more important, the tribal or national term emphasizes the important point that the descendants of the people who were in the Americas in 1492 are not one people. They were different people, nations, and tribes in 1492 and they still retain those differences in language and culture today. Even as today, those who pride themselves on their German heritage prefer to be referred to as "German" rather than something more general, such as European.

Distinguishing the Indians by their nation or tribal name also helps the reader understand that in the 1862 Dakota War, only two of the Dakota tribes fought in that war. Those two Dakota tribes, the Mdewakantons and the Wapekute, had their camps around the lower reservation and they constituted about 60% of the four Dakota tribes in Minnesota.

The term for the "other side" can be equally confusing. The persons in Minnesota who were attacked by the indigenous people were almost entirely descendants of recent immigrants from northern Europe, particularly Scandinavian and Germans. Some authors prefer terms such as "invader," "exploiter," "English" or even "conqueror." But it is hard to believe that Tore Olson, who never did speak English, saw himself as an invader or exploiter.

In this study I use the tribal group name, Dakota, or, where appropriate, the tribal name, Mdewakanton. For the others, I generally use the term of the person's occupation, such as farmer, settler, townsperson, or storekeeper. That gets a bit wordy at times, but it appears more neutral.

JRI

I

COMING TO MINNESOTA

She sat on the back porch and watched the sun rise over the gently rolling prairie of Alberta. It would be a warm day but now the sun felt good. Bullets and rifle butt had made her old body ache and the warmth of the sun helped. She rose slowly from her chair and with her cane—an irritating sign of growing old—she walked out to the back yard. August was a good time for the flowers and vegetables. Angus and Laura knew how to grow things—vegetables, fruit, and lots of flowers. They filled the back yard and Laura gave the bounty of her garden, particularly the flowers, to other people. Every wedding, funeral, and anniversary was likely to have the McDonnell's flowers.

She admired the roses, which were a specialty of Angus. He was a good son-in-law and a wonderful husband for Laura. Laura was her youngest and only daughter and she and Angus had opened their house to her.

She thought about her six children; she had stood at the graves of four of them and a grandson; mothers should not outlive their children. She walked up the gentle rise behind the farm buildings. The spring wheat covered the prairie land. The crop looked good, certainly better than it did last year in 1922.

She looked to the east. A hundred yards in front of her was a shallow depression filled with cattails, rushes and sedges. The Canadians, as did farmers in Minnesota, called them sloughs and they were usually too wet to cultivate.

She stood there quietly looking at the slough. She thought of the other slough a 1000 miles away and 60 years ago. If she stared, she could see her husband John and her sons, Frederick, Franklin, and Giles, dying and dead in that slough. The people in Minnesota now called it Slaughter Slough; she shuddered.

She turned and walked back to the white house. It was time. The battle for living had been a long struggle and it was time to let go.

Lavina Day Eastlick Smith Pettibone died at the age of 90 on October 9, 1923, in Lougheed, Alberta. A goodly number of her friends attended the funeral.

Lavina Day's "battle for living" began 2300 miles to the east. Colesville, in western New York, was a village of some 2400 residents when Lavina was born there on May 28, 1833. She was the youngest in a family of eleven. Her father, Giles, had been born in Vermont and was the sixth generation of Days who lived in Massachusetts and Vermont; they left Suffolk, England, in 1634. Her mother's (Hannah Culter) family had also lived in Massachusetts for six generations.

When Lavina was a year old, the family continued its journey west, settling in Trumbell County in eastern Ohio. Giles was a blacksmith and he remained there until his death in 1870. When Lavina was 15, she went with her brother Leicester, to Seneca County in central Ohio. There she met and married John Eastlick on June 13, 1850.

John Eastlick was born in 1823 in Ashtabula County, Ohio. His great grand-father, Alexander, had emigrated from Surrey, England, in the late 18th century. The family lived in New York and New Jersey.[1]

John's father moved to Ohio in the 1820s where John was born as the third youngest in a family of nine. Thus a fourth generation American married a fifth generation American and they moved westward with thousands of immigrants, seeking land to farm and homes for their families.

The westward trek of the Eastlick family can be traced by the birth places of their sons. Their first three (Merton,[2] 1851; Franklin, 1852; Giles, 1854) were born in Seneca County, Ohio.[3] In 1856, the family moved to Illinois where John believed he could obtain "a homestead cheaper." But land in Illinois was also too costly, so in 1857 they loaded up the wagon and came to Minnesota. In Ohio the Eastlicks had become friends with Tommy Ireland and his wife, Sophia, and their four daughters, Rosana, Ellen, Sarah Jane, and Julianne. They joined the Eastlicks on their move to Minnesota.

The Eastlicks first stopped in Olmsted County near Rochester. There Frederick (1857), William (1858)[4], and Johnnie (1861 in St. Charles) were born. Looking for even cheaper land, the Eastlicks and the Irelands moved to Murray County in western Minnesota.

The Eastlicks had leapfrogged over the somewhat orderly westward movement of settlers. This was not particularly unusual, but by settling in Murray County,

---

[1] The Eastlick name is spelled consistently, but there are differences in the historical records regarding Lavina Day. There are cases where her given name is "Lavinia" and her family name is spelled "Dat." But on official records, including her daughter Laura's birth certificate and census records her name is "Lavina" and her family name and her father's name is spelled "Day." The confusion apparently occurred because of Bryant and Murch's history of the Dakota War. In their book, published in 1864, they included Lavina's account, which she apparently sent them in manuscript form. Part of that account includes a brief biography that Lavina supplied. In that biography Lavina's last name is spelled "Dat" for herself and her father. This is likely a printing error because it is the only early account where her family name is spelled "Dat." But because Bryant and Murch's book received a wide circulation and still is a standard reference for the Dakota War, the misspelling was perpetuated. Eric Johansson, who worked on an unpublished account of Shetek, did an extensive genealogy of the Day/Eastlick family, including five geneations.

[2] In a few documents Merton is referred to as William Merton. His full name was Merton Ambrose Eastlick. Referring to Merton as William Merton may be a confusion with his brother, William who died as an infant. It may also be a confusion with Merton's own son, William Merton Eastlick (1874-1934). A Certificate of Death issued in 1986 by Olmsted Country continues the confusion by listing Merton as "Wm. M. Eastlick."

[3] An undocumented internet posted family history has the family moving to Indiana in 1854.

[4] Family tree information includes a William Eastlick who was born in 1858 in Olmsted County (Rochester) and who died the same year. There is no collaboration of that in birth or census records. John and his family are not included in the 1860 census in Rochester or in any of the townships near Rochester.

near Lake Shetek, they were putting some 50 miles between them and the edge of settlement in the western part of Brown County. New Ulm was the nearest town of any size and that was 70 miles east of Shetek. To the west, also some 70 miles, was the small community of Sioux Falls. The nearest group of soldiers was at Fort Ridgely, 50 miles east. But the land was cheap and the setting was attractive.[5]

But before the Eastlicks come to Shetek, both in terms of geography and settlement and in terms of story-making, there has to be a background.

Lake Shetek

Lake Shetek is one of a group of a dozen lakes in southwestern Minnesota. It and its companion lakes sit like jewels in the flat, somewhat featureless prairie that stretches to the Rocky Mountains. Lake Shetek at 1100 acres is the largest lake in that part of Minnesota. The Des Moines River flows out of the southern end of the lake, heads southeast into Iowa, and then transects the state on a diagonal until it empties into the Mississippi at Keokuk.

Shetek[6] is an Dakota word meaning either "pelican" for the birds that often nest there or "confluence of rivers" for the meeting of the Beaver Creek with the waters of the lake.

Today the area around the lake is more heavily forested than when the first white settlers began making homes there in the 1850s. The lake area was attractive to the Dakota who visited the lake for hundreds of years prior to the white contact. Some fur traders and trappers apparently also found the lake. For them and the settlers, the trees provided shelter and firewood, and game and fish were readily available. The trees also could be used for building material for the white settlers and the prairie that bordered the lake could be converted into farm land. The 1861 surveyor notes describe two sections near Lake Shetek:

> Township 107 N., Range 40: This township is partly of rolling and partly of level surface and of rich soil well adapted to cultivation except on the height of the prairie bluffs. The marshes are not all good for hay. The river bottom is of excellent soil but subject to overflow in high water. Des Moines River leaves the township in 36; its general course being a southeasterly one; small patches of ash, elm, and oak in some of the bends. And three large groves in sections 17 and 18; a mill dam formerly commenced is now going to be finished for the purpose of erecting a grist mill. Some good timber in the NE part of the township about the lakes, chiefly burr oaks, ash, elm, some cottonwood; also a

---

[5] Although Lavina describes John Eastlick seeking land to homestead, the Homestead Act did not go into effect until 1863. The land the Eastlicks looked for was probably preemption land. In this system, land could be settled before it was purchased or surveyed. When the surveyors laid out the land, the preemptor had the first choice to purchase the land. The land around Lake Shetek was surveyed in the fall of 1861. When Eastlick and the others came to this area, they would have preempted the land, and presumably purchase the land after the survey.

[6] Other spellings for the lake include Shetack, Shetesh, Chetek, Sheteik, Chetek, Chetoch, Shetareck.

little timber on Buffalo Lake. Smith and Everett claims are in sections 6 and 7. A few more claims are about to be made in sections 17 and 18. Surveyed September 14, 1861 by Lewis Brockman.

Township 108 N., Range 40: This township of good rich farming soil and of gently rolling partly level surface, is in its SE portion and in the north half entirely bare of timber and therefore not likely to be settled soon. But the southwest part of the same is very valuable having besides Lake Shetek several other lakes in its surrounding by excellent land and valuable timber forming beside, beautiful scenery. There are several settlers and fields to wit: Jones and Hurds on SE ¼ of section 20; a Kochs on south part of section 29; Palmerly on SE ¼ of section 32 and Meyers claim on North side of Lake Freemont. The island is claimed by M.T. Bee. To the following lakes on request of the settlers and by their agreement I have given names by which they are now passing among the settlers to wit, Lake Washburn, Lake Francis Siegel, Lake Fremont, and Bloody Lake. Surveyed October 8, 1861 by Lewis Brockman.[7]

In 1866, after the Shetek attack, Leonard Aldrich came to Shetek and settled with his family. They may have taken over the land formerly owned by Henry and Sophia Smith. In his letter Aldrich describes the land, climate and vegetation. Shetek clearly was a place that would have invited settlers in the mid-19th century.

Lake Shetek
June 3, 1866

Your very kind and welcome letter dated April 12 came to hand a few days ago. Was very glad to hear from you. I should have answered it before but our mail facilities are not very good. We only get it when we have a chance to send to New Ulm or in other words we only go seventy miles for our mail. Hannah and Clara start tomorrow for Castle Rock on a visit. Will be gone about a month. Joseph says tell Uncle Joseph that he wants to see you the most of any body that he knows of. We are all very pleasantly situated. Good land, a plenty of timber and water. The best chance for stock I ever saw. A chance for quite a settlement when the county is organized the county seat will be here. Men are in very thick looking for claims, all like very much, but this timber is so situated that all can get timber and prairie …some are preempting timber to sell out to the balance. Hannah likes it here much better than she used to at Castle Rock, Wild fruit is very abundant and a plenty of fish. I have sown 8 acres of wheat, planted about 18 acres of corn, and 2 ½ acres of potatoes. The boys are here and well suited. Our claims join, laying in an elbow of the lake, so one hundred and fifty rods of fence will enclose the three farms. Joseph has about fifty acres of timber on his place. Clarence has but little. I have enough on mine for fire wood. I have an island of about forty acres of good timber first rate red elm, white ash, white oak and bur oak are the principal variety of timber.

---

[7] The surveyor notes were compiled by William Trygg when he produced the "Composite Map of United States Land Surveyor's Original Plats and Field Notes" in the 1960s. The notes were transcribed from the original field notes of the surveyors. Trygg's collection is part of the archives of the Minnesota Historical Society.

Joseph has a few hard maples on his. Wild plums and gooseberries by the acres, black raspberries in abundance. The nearest way to get here would be to come direct from [O]watona to Mankato. From Mankato to Leavenworth. Then to Lake Shetek. I wish you could come up here and make us a visit if nothing more we are having a very growing times now. Frequent showers every thing is looking finely. I am in hope to have a mail route established through here before long. Then I can answer our letters more promptly. I shall go to St. Peters the 20th of June, shall expect an answer to this then. First to New Ulm. Give my best regards to grandpa and Grand Ma Farkherst. I would like to see them very much. My love to Martha and the girls. I want to see them all more than I can express. How I wish I could see you all this evening. We are all well and have been since we came here.[8] (Aldrich 1866)

Explorers and fur traders would have been the first whites at Lake Shetek; George Catlin, the painter, may have passed near Shetek on his way to Pipestone. By 1860 Lake Shetek had become a small community of settlers.

---

[8]   Aldrich, Leonard. 1866 Letter to Brother, June 3. Aldrich Papers, Minnesota Historical Society Archives. Minnesota Historical Society, St. Paul, MN

II

The Shetek Trail

… this half-mile or so within the pasture fence was all that was left of that old road which used to run like a wild thing across the open prairie, clinging to the high places and circling and doubling like a rabbit before the hounds.

Willa Cather's description of a prairie trail in Nebraska (*My Antonia*) could easily be applied to the Shetek Trail. This trail was an important part of the accounts of the Shetek survivors and it served as a vital connection between Shetek and civilization. The Shetek Trail, as other trails, probably followed paths known and used by the Indians, who in turn may have followed trails used by deer or other animals. (See Plates 1, 2.)

A well-known trail, sometimes called the "Military Trail" or the "Nobles Trail"[9] in southern Minnesota, went from Fort Ridgely to the Missouri River. The following is a description of the route:

> This road was completed only as far as the Missouri river, 254 miles, some time in the fall of 1857, in consequence of the insufficiency of the appropriation and of alleged Indian hostilities. The general location of this road is as follows: Beginning at the ferry on the Minnesota river, which is 150 feet wide at this place, opposite Fort Ridgely. The general course of the road is southwesterly, passing through a marshy region a few miles south of Limping Devil's lake to the north fork of the Cottonwood, a distance of about seventeen miles, thence to the Cottonwood river, over a rolling country, with lakes and marshes, about one and one-half miles below the mouth of Plum Creek [Walnut Grove today], and three good watering places to the crossing of Cottonwood at Big Wood, about eighteen and one-half miles. Thence the road continues to Hole-in-the-Mountain, near Lake Benton, a distance of about thirty-two miles, passing through a region abounding in lakes and an abundance of wood, water and grass. From Lake Benton the road passes for the most part over a high prairie to the Big Sioux river, about twenty-three and one-half miles.[10]

The Nobles road went north of Lake Shetek, generally following US Hwy 14, and crossed the Minnesota border near Lake Benton. This was a major east-west

---

9   The Nobles Trail got its name from Colonel William H. Nobles, a well-known explorer. He is credited with discovering a pass in the Rockies which shortened the emigrant route. Nobles County in Southwestern Minnesota was named after him.

10   Campbell, Albert, H., General Superintendent. Report of the Secretary of the Interior, communicating Reports upon the Pacific Wagon Roads constructed under the direction of that Department. February 23, 1859. Senate. 35th Congress, 2d Session. Ex. Doc. No. 36.

trail, particularly for pioneers or military forces moving westward.[11] The Pembina trail between the Red River and St. Paul was another well-known and mapped trail.

The Post Road

The Mail Route from New Ulm to Sioux Falls, the proper name of the Shetek Trail, was authorized on February 26, 1857 by the U.S. Congress through a memorial from the Minnesota Territorial Legislature. The authorization provided for "the establishment of certain Mail Routes." Three such routes were authorized in Minnesota: (1) An extension of the mail route from New Ulm via Cornwell City to Sioux Falls City, (2) from Mankato via South Bend along the south side of the Minnesota River to New Ulm, and (3) from New Ulm to the town of Jackson.[12]

The memorial gave as the reason for these routes the "large and increasing settlements in the Territory."[13]

There is no town of "Cornwell City" in southwestern Minnesota nor was there ever such a town. The name is fictitious but its inclusion in the enabling resolution tells something about the Minnesota Territory and its politics in 1857.

[11] A document in the Workman Papers also describes the route of the trail from Fort Ridgely to the Missouri and gives several other names for the trail: the "Nobles Trail" after the surveyor, and the "Fort Ridgely and South Pass Road." Several period maps, including A.J. Johnson's Minnesota Map c. 1865, show several branches of this military trail. The town of New Brunswick, which no longer exists, in section 8, Highwater Township, Cottonwood County appears to be a dividing place between trails. The Military Trail heads in a north northeasterly direction at New Brunswick crossing the Big Cottonwood near Lamberton, Redwood County. The Shetek Trail however continues in an east northeast direction staying on the south side of the Big Cottonwood. Another fork in the Military Trail occurred at Saratoga, another town that no longer exists, a bit northwest of Tracy in Lyon County, or on some maps, to the northwest of Balaton. The 1858 A.J. Hill Sectional Map also indicates several branching routes of various trails. It shows a trail, which comes out of Fort Ridgely (the Military Trail) with a branch to the Lower Agency, heads southwesterly to New Brunswick and then continues on to Shetek using what later became the Shetek Trail. From there it went through Pipestone County following Flandreau Creek into South Dakota where it ends at Sioux Falls. It would appear that the Military Trail precedes the Shetek Trail and the three men who later plotted the Shetek Trail may have used the Military Trail in Pipestone and Murray County.

[12] Congress took up a number of bills authorizing post routes in Minnesota in 1857-1859 e.g., "Resolved, That the Committee on Post Offices and Post Roads be instructed to inquire into the expediency of establishing a post route from Fort Dodge, Iowa, to Jackson, in Minnesota; and a post route from Jackson, Minnesota, to Sioux Falls, in Dacotah Territory; and a semi-monthly mail from New Ulm, in said State, (Minnesota,) to Jackson, in Minnesota." *Journal of the Senate*, January 19, 1859. "Resolved, That the Committee on Post Offices and Post Roads be instructed to inquire into the expediency of establishing the following post routes in the State of Minnesota: From Owatoma, in Steele county, via Clear Lake and Josco, to Mankato, in Blue Earth county; from Austin, in Mercer county, via Geneva, Berlin, Otisco, Wilton, and Josco, to St. Peters, in Nicollet county; from Austin to Blue Earth City; from New Ulm, via Tuttle's Farm, to Leavenworth; from St. Cloud, via Brottenburg and Brunswick, to Fortuna; from Faribault, in Rice county, to Wilton, in Waseca county; from Grey Eagle, via Pine Creek P.O., to Ridgeway; from Rochester, via Salem, Ashland, and Somerset, to Wilton; from Fort Dodge, in Iowa, via Emmett City, thence to Odessa, in Minnesota, thence, via Cresco, Crystal Lake City, to Mankato." *Journal of the Senate*, May 21, 1858.

[13] Session Laws of the Territory of Minnesota, passed by the Legislative Assembly at the Eighth Session, commencing January 7, 1857. St. Paul: Earle Goodrich, Territorial Printer, 1857.

Minnesota was moving into statehood in 1857. Inkpaduta had raided southwestern Minnesota that year and the army failed to capture him. In that same year a five million dollar congressional land grant was given to Minnesota for building railroads. That sparked a land boom in southern Minnesota. But to obtain statehood and increase the inflow of settlers who would buy the land and use the future railroads, the movers and shakers in Minnesota had to demonstrate there was a population, particularly in southwestern Minnesota, and it was a safe place to settle.

An election had been called for October 1857 to ratify the new state constitution and to elect members of the national House of Representatives and state officials, including a governor. A census was also required by the enabling act before Minnesota could be accepted as a state. This census was conducted in October 1857. The Democrats were in a desperate contest with the new Republican party and each had its own agenda and slate of candidates. Henry Sibley was the gubernatorial candidate for the Democrats and Alexander Ramsey was the candidate for the Republicans. The Territorial Legislature, which was strongly Democratic, sent the mail routes memorial to Congress in January, and included a city (Cornwell) that did not exist. In that same special session the legislature established seven counties in southwestern Minnesota: Martin, Jackson, Nobles, Cottonwood, Murray, Rock, and Pipestone. Most of these new counties had few or no settlers, but the legislature set up paper towns, such as Sulphur Springs and Bad Track in Cottonwood County, Council City and Oasis in Murray County, Wakeeta in Rock County, and Gretchtown in Nobles County.[14] Cornwell City also appeared, sometimes misspelled as Conwell City or Council City, in Murray County. But these paper towns also needed a population who could vote and be counted in the application for statehood.

That was not a problem because the 1857 census in October would supply those mythical people for those mythical towns. The 1857 census in Murray County didn't include anyone around Lake Shetek but it did show a Parker Anderson, 35 years old, from North Carolina, working as a blacksmith in Cornwell City. With him were 91 other residents, with an impressive range of skills and occupations: a millwright, a brick layer, a miller, a sawyer, a saddler, a physician, a plasterer, a hotel keeper, two wagon makers, a grocer, a baker, a shoe maker, and two carpenters, plus 17 laborers and 16 farmers. There were also 23 children, just enough for a school. This was a thriving community, and none of it was real. (See Plates 3 & 4.)

The census in southwestern Minnesota was conducted by Nathanial R. Brown, the brother of Joseph R. Brown, well-known trader and Democrat. The U.S. Marshal for Minnesota, William Gere, certified that he "carefully examined and compared the returns of the census of Murray County and that the same are correct." Even more impressive, these mythical residents in these mythical towns

---

[14]   Forrest, Robert J. Mythical Cities of Southwestern Minnesota. *Minnesota History.* Vol. 14, #3, 1933. 243-262

voted to the man for the Democratic candidates, including Sibley who won the governorship by 240 votes.[15]

Although Cornwell did not exist, it was placed on maps where Currie, Murray County, today is located. When the 1857 act setting up the mail routes was adopted, the presence of Cornwell on the maps would place the New Ulm to Sioux Falls road passing just south of Lake Shetek. The town existed long enough to shape the route of the trail.

The Shetek Trail, and it has different names depending on a particular location of part of the trail, does not appear on many maps or atlases of the 1860s. Part of the trail is shown on the A. J. Johnson 1865 map (Plate 6). On this map the trail angles northeast in Cottonwood County, crosses the Big Cottonwood west of Sanborn, goes north of Sleepy Eye and then northeast to the Fort. West of Lake Shetek, it goes to the southwest through Pipestone, west to the Minnesota border and then south to Sioux Falls. Folwell shows this trail but there is no label.[16] This trail, particularly because it branches near Sanborn, appears to be the Fort Ridgely to the Missouri River trail or the Military Trail (Plate 2).

The Shetek Trail is best seen in the 1861 surveyor maps. These maps were drawn by the original surveyors of the land, who worked in southwestern Minnesota in various years between 1858 and 1872, generally from east to west. Their work included field notes describing the land and a map for each township in the county, showing land features such as rivers, lakes, and swamps and the lines indicating the sections of land in the township. The range and township numbers were included as well as the latitude and longitude. The maps were essential in the sale and taxing of the land.

The western terminus of the post road was Sioux Falls. That is not surprising considering the background of Sioux Falls and one of the land companies, the Dakota Land Company, that promoted the settlement of Sioux Falls. Joseph Nicolai Nicollet in 1839 had explored the picturesque falls of the Big Sioux River, called by the Yanktonais Indians as "Te-han-kas-an-data" (Thick-wooded-river). George Staples of Dubuque also explored the region in 1856 and was struck by the potential for water power in the rapids and falls. He organized the Western Town Company of Dubuque to settle and develop the area.[17] They established a claim for 320 acres at the falls and set up the town. At the same time, the Dakota Land Company was chartered by the Territorial Legislature of Minnesota for the purpose of determining future locations of towns in the western part of the Minnesota Territory. Minnesota had applied for statehood, which it received in 1858, but until the western boundary of Minnesota was set by Congress, the land

---

[15] Payback time came in 1860, when the real census was taken by the federal government and a new election was held. The mythical towns disappeared with their mythical inhabitants and the Republicans wiped the floor with the Democrats, winning both state and federal offices.

[16] Folwell, William Watts. 1956. *A History of Minnesota* Vol. I. St. Paul, MN: Minnesota Historical Society.

[17] The officers of the company included Dr. J. M. Staples, Mayor Hetherington of Dubuque, Dennis Mahoney, Austin Adams, George Waldron, William Tripp, W.W. Brookings, Dr. J. L. Philips. (Kingsbury, George W. 1915. *History of the Dakota Territory, Vol. 1.* Chicago: S.J. Clarke Publishing Co.)

east of the Big Sioux, including Sioux Falls, was part of Minnesota. The incorporators of the Dakota Land Company included familiar names: Joseph Brown, his two half brothers, Nathaniel and Samuel F. Brown, S.A. Medary (territorial governor), and Charles Flandrau. The representatives of the company left St. Paul in the spring of 1857, and followed the Nobles trail to the Big Sioux River. There they pre-located a town, Medary, named after the governor and incorporator of the company. This was intended to be the capital of the new territory of Dakota.[18] Following the Big Sioux south, the representatives established the town of Flandrau, named for Charles Flandrau. This town also failed to become a reality. Any settlers there abandoned the town in 1862 and it remained deserted until 1869 when some Santee Indians who wanted to forsake the reservation life left the Santee Reservation near Niobrara, Nebraska, moved into the area and settled as homesteaders.[19] In a footnote to an introduction to an article on Sioux Falls, Charles Flandrau noted, with a touch of regret, that the name of the town was and still is misspelled as "Flandreau."[20] From there the company representatives went south to the falls where they found another land company, the Western Town Company. The Dakota Land Company also staked out a land claim and opened an office for the sale of land. The two land companies remained friendly rivals. Most of the representatives of the Dakota Land Company returned to St. Paul after establishing land offices in Saratoga and Lake Benton.

The mail route between New Ulm and Sioux Falls could have been suggested by the Dakota Land Company. In a report they made in 1859, they listed places and the location of these places where the company had or planned to have land offices. Some of the following could have been locations that were intended to be connected by the New Ulm to Sioux Falls route:

- Saratoga: county seat of Cottonwood County on Big Cottonwood River, 60 miles west of New Ulm at the bridge crossing of the Nobles Road.
- Mountain Pass: head of Lake Benton
- Medary: Big Sioux River at Government Road crossing, 25 miles west of the Mountain Pass.
- Flandrau: 15 miles from Medary, on the Big Sioux River
- Emaniji: 13 miles before the Falls, where the Big Sioux River and Split Rock River meet, head of navigation.
- Lynd: Brown County, Redwood River, Bad Track's Indian Village.

---

[18] The town was never incorporated and as a result of the Dakota War in Minnesota, all white settlers left the area and the town disappeared. Later the town was reestablished, but failed again and finally, when the railroad went through, the town was moved six miles north and renamed Brookings.

[19] See Allen, Clifford, et al. 1971. History of the Flandreau Santee Sioux Tribe. Unpublished manuscript.

[20] Albright, Samuel (with a preface by Judge Charles E. Flandrau). 1898. "The First Organized Government of Dakota." *Collections of the Minnesota Historical Society,* Vol VIII. St. Paul: The Society. Pp.127-149.

- Redwood and Redwood Center: on Redwood River at the crossing of the New Ulm route.
- Ressane (?) 20 miles north of Medary
- Great Oasis: on the mail route to New Ulm.[21]

The Dakota Land Company was successful in inducing the Territorial Legislature to petition Congress for a mail route that would connect unsettled land in western Minnesota and eastern Dakota Territory with eastern Minnesota, land that they could sell.[22]

The government contracted in 1861 with three persons to lay out a mail route which followed the route stipulated in the authorizing legislation. (Plate 9) One of the surveyors of the route was an early settler in Murray County, Hoel Parmlee (or Parmerlee). The other two were a lawyer and a one-eyed "Old Steve" from Dubuque.

The route of that trail in South Dakota remains uncertain. The survey map for Sioux Falls, drawn in 1860, indicates a road going north out of Sioux Falls. Because the Big Sioux curves around Sioux Falls on three sides, only to the north can a road be made without crossing the Big Sioux River. Early accounts of Sioux Falls tell of a road which was constructed to Medery (Medary), but the road is not labeled on any survey maps for South Dakota; there are township maps which may have a trail indicated (Twnshp102;R49, Twnshp103:R49; Twnshp107:R47), but this may also be a land elevation mark. These survey maps were drawn after the Dakota War, in the late 1860s. Persons familiar with the early history of the Sioux Falls believe the mail route went northeast rather than north out of Sioux Falls. They contend the trail followed the Split Rock Creek which enters South Dakota near Sherman, SD and then through Jasper, MN up to Pipestone. This is also the route of the Burlington Northern railroad. The map that Folwell used in his history also suggests that the trail angled down to Sioux Falls after leaving Pipestone.[23] Additional support for the Split Rock Creek route is found in a report of a journey from Sioux Falls to Pipestone by surveyors in October 1864. They describe their route as "passing around the long bend [of the Big Sioux River] and turned our way eastward for the Split Rock river," which they then followed to the Pipestone River.[24]

The surveys in the Dakota Territory were made in the late 1860s and the New Ulm to Sioux Falls Trail had likely been abandoned by then, at least in the

---

[21] Report of the Dakota Land Company, *The Dakota Democrat*, November 8, 1859

[22] There are, confusingly, some records that suggest the trail or road did not go to New Ulm. Kingsbury (1915, 106) indicates that Sioux Falls had postal facilities as early as 1858, about the time Congress authorized the trail, but the city received mail twice a month from Henderson, Minnesota. Byron Smith was the postmaster. About March 1, 1859, a change was made when the mail service was transferred from Henderson to Sioux City, which increased the mail service to once a week by a man on horseback. Perhaps the route did go through New Ulm and then to Henderson, but that seems unlikely.

[23] Folwell, W. F. *A History of Minnesota,* Vol 1. St. Paul: Minnesota Historical Society, 1956, p. 81.

[24] Armstrong, Moses K. 1901. *The Early Empire Builder of the Great West..* St. Paul: Pioneer Press, p. 158

Dakota Territory, because most of the settlers had fled from Sioux Falls because of the Indian attacks. Already in 1864 a group of traders traveled the mail route between Yankton and Sioux falls and they described it as "now overgrown with grass."[25] In addition, the surveyors did not generally examine the land inside the section lines, which they had the responsibility for establishing. They may have missed any trail indications.

The post road becomes more evident in Pipestone County in the townships between the Minnesota border and the city of Pipestone and then east from Pipestone into the first township range (43) in Murray County. The second and third township ranges (42, 41) do not indicate the trail. The supposition of the local historians, based on knowledge of the land formation in those ranges, suggests that the trail went through the Great Oasis area and then to the southern end of Lake Shetek, where it is again labeled on the surveyor maps. The Great Oasis had a trading post and it was listed as one of the proposed land offices; it is likely that the mail route went through the Great Oasis.

The Great Oasis was an area of shallow lakes, numerous streams, and tall prairie grass. It was also a trappers' paradise, filled with fox, otter, beaver, mink, and muskrats. Joseph LaFramboise had established a trading post as part of the American Fur Company near or in the Great Oasis. The trading post was abandoned in 1837 and burned by the Dakota the next year. The Great Oasis no longer exists; it was drained in the 1910s.

On the Murray Township surveyor map (Twnshp 107:R40) the trail is clearly labeled as the Sioux Falls to New Ulm Trail. After passing south of Lake Shetek, it follows the route described in Lavina Eastlick's account. Plate 5 shows an 1861 surveyor map with the 36 sections in Murray Township. On the upper left is Lake Shetek. A trail is shown passing south of Lake Shetek, then easterly keeping south of a large slough (probably Slaughter Slough, sections 2, 3, 10, 11) and then angling southeast to Buffalo Lake (section 12). The trail is labeled as the "Road to Sioux Falls" and "South Road from Lake Shetek to New Ulm." The map was obviously drawn after the Shetek Trail had been laid out.

Dovay Township (Twnshp 107:R39) also shows the labeled post road, passing north of Buffalo Lake and angling north into the southeastern corner of Holly Township (Townshp 108:R39) (Plate 9). When it enters Cottonwood County (Ann Township, Twnshp108:R38), the trail is not marked or indicated.

Recently, a resident of Highwater Township (Twnshp108:R37) in Cottonwood County researched and traced the Shetek Trail in that township.[26] Dr. Daryl Batalden traced the trail based on his own recollections as a child and current observations of ruts in unplowed land. According to the map which accompanied the article, the Shetek Trail went in a northeasterly direction through Highwater

[25]   Armstrong, 1901, p. 158

[26]   *Lamberton News*, February 5, 1997, page 8. The article refers to the trail as the "military trail." There is also a confusion because the article refers to this trail as being used in 1862 by the 62 refugees which fled from the Upper Agency. This group, which consisted of persons from the Riggs and Williamson missions who were guided by John Otherday, traveled on the north side of the Minnesota River, miles from the New Ulm to Sioux Falls Trail.

Township. Batalden, however, put Dutch Charley's cabin on Highwater Creek, and located the dugout on a farm owned by a relative, Reuben Batalden. Dutch Charley, however, had his cabin on the creek named for him, "Dutch Charley Creek," which is five miles to the southwest of the indicated crossing and cabin site on Highwater Creek. This misplacement of Dutch Charley's cabin doesn't necessarily mean Batalden did not identify the trail, but it does indicate the difficulties in accurately locating the trail. Somewhere near Dutch Charley's cabin, was the proposed town of New Brunswick. It may have been here that the route divided. One section went north-northeast and crossed the Cottonwood near the present town of Lamberton. From there it joined the military trial to Fort Ridgely. The other route stayed on the south side of the Cottonwood and continued on to New Ulm. (Plate 7)

By extrapolating from that drawing, the trail went through Germantown Township (Twnshp108:R36) in an easterly direction until it left Cottonwood County and entered Brown County in the northwest corner of Stately Township (Twnshp108:R35). From there is may have angled slightly north, passing briefly into North Star Township (Twnshp 109:R35) keeping to the south side of the Big Cottonwood. The trail would then likely have gone through Burnstown Township (Twnshp 109:R34), south of the present city of Springfield. The road passed the homestead of Jonathan Brown (T109:R34-W, Sec 22, NW ¼ of NW ¼), a young man of 37 who lived with his 71-year old father, Joseph, and his 30-year old sister, Horatia, on the Cottonwood River just east of Springfield. The site of this house, or "stopping place," is known, as well as the place where the family was killed (T109:R33-W, Sec 28, SW ¼ of S ½ of NW ¼). The survivors traveling the Shetek road typically mentioned either the Brown house or the bodies of the Browns. Lavina Eastlick included in her account that the bodies of the Brown family were five miles east of their cabin, near a little "run." There are several small creeks that are crossed by CH24. One of them is about ¾ a mile from the present village of Leavenworth. This creek is also five miles east of the Brown cabin. In addition, a long-time local resident, Ed Kolbe, claimed that artifacts from the Brown wagon had been found years ago at that site.

From there the road continued on to the present village of Leavenworth, and there it is sometimes called the Leavenworth Trail. At this point it is not clear just where the Shetek/Leavenworth Trail went. Between Leavenworth and New Ulm there are four or five trails. There was a Reservation Trail that went from New Ulm, following CR 27 to the eastern boundary of the Dakota Reservation, then going directly south and crossing the Big Cottonwood, or it followed the north side of the Big Cottonwood to present-day Leavenworth, where it crossed the Cottonwood at Jackson Crossing. There may also be a crossing in Sigel Township.

Another version of the Shetek Trail appears to have followed CR 24 south of School Lake in Sigel Township where it angled to the northeast, south of Clear Lake, up through Cottonwood Township and entered New Ulm from the south. The trail could have entered New Ulm either by following a ravine down to the Cottonwood River and crossing at a place about ½ mile from the current State

Fig. 1   Bridge over the Cottonwood River
In the early 20th century this bridge was south of New Ulm. It connected Bridge Street in New Ulm with Shag Road (on the left). It may be the ford where the Sioux Falls to New Ulm route crossed the Cottonwood.

Highway 15 bridge. Another route would have taken the Shetek Trail along the bluff south of New Ulm, crossing State Highway 15 and going down to the Cottonwood on what is called Shag Road (Plate 8). This would be about a mile before the Cottonwood enters the Minnesota. The trail would have crossed the Cottonwood and connected to Bridge Street in New Ulm. In the early 20th century there was a bridge here that connected Bridge Street to Shag road.

The evidence for where the Shetek Trail went into New Ulm is still slim. There was a trail from New Ulm to Mankato, which generally followed State Highway 66. There are some 19th century maps that show two routes into New Ulm, one down the ravine described above and the other along what is today called Shag Road, and there are stories from landowners of trails and fords in those two areas. There is also an account by the party of Aaron Myers, Bently, William Everett, and Charlie Hatch, all from Shetek, who made it into New Ulm from the south. They were chased by the Dakota down the bluff during the Saturday attack on New Ulm. Either the Shag Road or the ravine could have been a route of that flight.

In Leavenworth and Sigel Townships there are landowners whose land has been farmed for several generations of their family. They have stories told them about where the Shetek Trail, or some other trail, crossed their land. For example, in section 15 of Sigel Township, Lakeside Road passes between a small lake (just east of School Lake) and a slough. The landowner, Leo Guggisberg, affirms that this road follows the Old Shetek Trail.

When the trails were laid out they were marked with stakes, particularly in winter, and where the trail crossed a creek or river, the banks were roughly cut down and logs were laid across the creek to provide a crude (and temporary) bridge for wagons. Nobles notes that he built a "rough" bridge on the Cottonwood River, which was improved and was described as the "finest bridge on the [Nobles/Military] road."[27] He also built a camp near the Cottonwood River crossing consisting of a stable, a log cabin, and a garden.

The farmers needed the Shetek Trail and other trails to bring their crops and produce to towns where they could be sold or bartered for food, clothing, and tools. The journey between Shetek and New Ulm took some four to six days and typically the farmers would join together with their wagons on this semi-annual trip. The Shetek farmers also could have taken their produce to Fort Ridgely by branching to the northeast near the New Brunswick fork. The Shetek trail was

27   Rice, Arthur. 1912. *An Illustrated History of Lyon County Minnesota.* Marshall, MN: Northern History Publishing Co.

also a mail route and a marked road for persons traveling west. Mail carriers used a small carriage, sometimes called a surrey or a hack. Mail regulations allowed a mail carrier to accommodate one or two passengers in his carriage.

The trail or road between Sioux Falls and New Ulm was a route that clearly was used. The Sioux Falls newspaper in 1859 carried an advertisement for a hotel in New Ulm:

> Dakota House, Minnesota Street
> Seiter & Erd Proprietors
> This new hotel contains a number of spacious and airy rooms. Terms:
> One dollar per day. Single meals 25 cents. Good stabling attached.[28]

The proprietors would not have placed the ad unless they also believed that some residents of Sioux Falls would make their way to New Ulm and need lodging.

The New Ulm to Sioux Falls mail route had a short life. On August 25, 1862, a well-known citizen of Sioux Falls, Judge John. B. Amidon, and his son, William, were killed in a hay field near Sioux Falls[29] and a few days later news reached Sioux Falls of the Dakota War in Minnesota. Sioux Falls was hastily abandoned and shortly after the departure of the settlers, the Yanktonais burned the village. For nearly three years the Big Sioux Valley remained deserted.[30] This effectively ended the New Ulm to Sioux Falls mail route, although the trail existed and mail may have been sent to other places on the trail, there was no need to send mail to Sioux Falls. Later other trails and roads were constructed particularly those south of the original trail that served Sioux City and eastern Dakota Territory.

But some remnants of the trail existed. Sometime in late 1863 a detachment of the Sixth Minnesota Volunteer Regiment under the command of J. C. Whitney, escorted a supply train from Mankato to Fort Thompson, Dakota Territory. They followed the New Ulm to Sioux Falls mail route until Pipestone. The report is very detailed in what they saw, the rivers and creeks they crossed, and where camped. The report is given below, beginning at Leavenworth where they joined the mail route from Mankato. Comments within the brackets give current place names.

> Leavenworth is a well-selected town site on the northern bank of the Big Cottonwood river,[31] about forty miles west of Mankato, and fifteen miles from New Ulm. Like many other western towns, its proprietors exceed its population.
> Yet it was here the last smoke of a white settler met our eyes, until reaching the agency on the Missouri river. [Fort Thompson]

---

[28] *The Dakota Democrat,* December 15, 1859

[29] The leader of the band which killed the Amidons was said to have been Inkpaduta. Smith, Charles. 1949. *A Comprehensive History of Minnehaha County, South Dakota.* Mitchell, SD: Educator Supply Co.

[30] Bailey, Dana R. 1899. *History of Minnehaha County, South Dakota.* Sioux Falls: Brown and Saenger.

[31] Today, Leavenworth is on the south side of theCottonwood River.

From our camp on the opposite bank of the river, which we lett on the morning of the 16th of November, we moved up the stream, keeping near its banks for a distance of five miles; then diverging and leaving it from one to four miles to our right, we passed over rich rolling prairie for ten miles, when we came upon a series of high gravel knolls, much like the Coteau de Missouri, but not so abrupt as to compel us to change our course.

Two miles further on, at a bend of the Cottonwood, we found a good camp ground near the mouth of Mound creek, a beautiful little stream of good water, abounding in fish, wood, and grass in abundance. [Northstar Tnshp, Brown County]

The creek being crossed without difficulty, we passed over high uneven prairie for two miles, when we came upon a rich undulating country, and seven miles brought us to Dry creek, (a misnomer, there being plenty of water,) upon whose banks were a few scattering trees and kinnekinnick. Crossed without difficulty or delay. [Germantown Twnshp, Cottonood County]

Four miles from this we came to Old creek, a small, clear stream, easily crossed and well timbered. [Not certain, probably Highwater in Highwater Twnshp, Cottonwood County]

Four miles of rich, level prairies, and we came to the town-site of New Brunswick, on Charles creek, [Dutch Charley Creek, Ann Twnshp, Cottonwood County] where were two or three log-buildings and other improvements, which the merciless hands of savages had made desolate.

The banks of Charles creek are from fifty to seventy-five feet above its bed, but at the point of crossing they are of so gradual slope that the heavy-burdened teams found no difficulty in crossing. There is an abundance of timber upon this stream, viz., white ash, cottonwood, and basswood.

The ascent of its opposite bank brought us upon a broad, level prairie, with a dark, rich soil. Seven miles in a direction little south of west we came to the northern extremity of Long lake; [Dovray Twnshp, Murray County, now just a lakebed] good water and grass, but no wood. From this point the land it more rolling. Five miles further on is a beautiful sheet of water, from one to one and a half mile in extent, known as Buffalo lake, upon the banks of which are some scattering trees, cottonwood and ash. [Dovray Twnshp, Murray County]

Six miles more of rolling prairie brought us to the Des Moines river, at the foot of Lake Sheteck [sic]. [Murray Twnshp, Murray County]

The rich farming lands, timber, and water power, had induced several families to make their homes here previous to the Indian massacres; but some having been killed, others captured, and the remainder driven oft', it is again desolate, and the once happy homes, now ruined and abandoned, are all that is left of civilization.

After fording the Des Moines, a mile below the lake, we crossed ten miles of rolling prairie, and came to Beaver creek, a small, muddy stream running south from the Great Oasis, a timbered marsh and lake three miles above. [Mason/Lowville Twnshp, Murray County, the Great Oasis was drained in the 1910s.]

Our general course up to this time had been about ten degrees south of west, and nearly on the old trail leading from New Ulm to Sioux Falls, on the Big Sioux river.

Bearing a little more south for three miles, to avoid low, marshy ground, we then took a course nearly west.

A continuation of rich, rolling prairie for twelve miles, and three miles of hilly country, brought us to Rock river; near its source a small, clear, running stream of pure water; no timber in the vicinity. [Burke Twnshp, Pipestone County]

The country from this point to Big Sioux river is alternately rolling and level.

Two miles from our crossing the Rock river we crossed a branch of the same.

Ten miles further on we came to the consecrated ground of the Dakota, the red pipestone quarry; also crossed Pipestone creek.[Sweet Twnshp, Pipestone County]

Twelve miles from here, after making a gradual descent of the high bluff, and crossing a mile of intervening flat, we came to the Big Sioux. [Clair Twnshp, Moody County, SD?]

The stream is from two to three rods wide; crossing excellent, water not exceeding one foot in depth; gravel bottom and low banks.

From here the expedition continued to Fort Thompson, on the Missouri River. A mileage chart (see Table 1) was also included in the report (all miles from Mankato).

Today, however, there are few if any physical traces of the 1860 trails. The trails themselves probably have been moved or erased when the land was surveyed and cultivated. The law at that time allowed farmers to put up fences blocking the trails and forcing travelers to follow section lines. Thus, they became parts of township roads which follow section lines today. Also, when a county road replaced a trail, as might have happened in CR24, the trail would have been obliterated by the grading and surfacing of the new road.

Thus, can a traveler walk the trails today? In some parts, yes, but in most parts it would be a best guess.

The accompanying map (Plate 9) is one of those "best guesses." It was constructed by placing the original surveyor maps on a large Adobe Illustrator Document, 32 inches by 16 inches. There were 118 survey maps placed, each map showing a township, for a total of 4248 sections or square miles. The map encompasses a section of Minnesota and South Dakota 126 miles long and 60 miles wide. When a surveyor township map indicated the New Ulm to Sioux Falls Trail, a red solid line was drawn tracing the trail. In Cottonwood County, Highwater Township, the research done by Dr. Batalden was used to identify the trail. Where there was no trail indicated on the survey map, or in the instances where there were no surveyor maps available, a dotted line was drawn showing the best extrapolation of the trail. The surveyor maps were also used to trace the rivers and lakes shown on the map. To reduce the size of the digital file, the surveyor maps that did not include the route of the New Ulm to Sioux Falls Trail were deleted.

Table 1
Places and mileage on the 1863
expedition

Place	Miles
Mankato	
Leavenworth	40
Mound creek	57
Dry creek	66
Old creek	70
New Brunswick	74
Long lake	81
Buffalo lake	85
Lake Sheteck	91
Beaver creek	101
Rock river	119
Pipe stone quarry	131
Big Sioux river	143

The Postman

Although the route authorized by Congress went from New Ulm to Sioux Falls, Sioux Falls was not the western terminus of the postal service in the late 1850s and early 1860s in the Dakota Territory. When Minnesota was granted statehood in 1858, the establishment of its western border left what is now eastern South Dakota, from the Missouri River east to that border, in kind of a limbo. It was still officially part of the Minnesota Territory which really didn't exist because of Minnesota statehood while the Dakota Territory wasn't established until three years later in 1861. The settlers east of the Missouri River therefore took matters in their own hands and elected a territorial legislature, but had difficulty in getting their representative to Congress seated.[32] There was, however, a post office established in 1859 in Sioux Falls. The first postmaster was James Allen and it was located in the Dakota Land Company's building in Sioux Falls.

The 1860 federal census, however, shows Sioux City as the postoffice for Sioux Falls and most of the other enumeration districts in the soon-to-be-established Dakota Territory had Sioux City also as their postoffice. Sioux Falls, with a total census population of 38, was one of the smaller districts in the census. The Yankton Agency to the west had a population of nearly 500 and Vermillion, between Yankton and Sioux Falls, had a population of 230. Sioux City in Iowa had a population of nearly 900. There may have been several mail routes in the area.

---

32   Bailey, Dana.1899. *The History of Minnehaha County, South Dakota.* Sioux Falls: Brown & Saenger Printers.

Routing all the mail from Sioux City and all the settlements on the Big Sioux River through New Ulm, Mankato, and Winona doesn't appear to make sense. The mail from Yankton, Vermillion, and Sioux Falls may have been transported through Sioux Falls to New Ulm and then to points east. A likely alternate would be that the mail from all the settlements, except Sioux Falls, went directly to Sioux City and then east to Dubuque or Davenport. In that arrangement the mail route from Sioux Falls to New Ulm was designed to collect and deliver the mail in western Minnesota, as the original petition suggests, and deliver it to New Ulm where it would continue to the east through Mankato, Owatonna, Rochester, and Winona. Pipestone, for example had a census population in 1860 of 23 and their mail was likely picked up by the post man on his route to New Ulm.[33] Support for this arrangement was the military road from Sioux City to Fort Randall that was laid out in 1856. This road, complete with bridges or ferries over the James and Vermillion rivers, provided supplies and a route for military personnel to the forts along the Missouri River. It was also used as a mail route for the growing communities of Vermillion and Yankton.[34]

A mail route presumes a mailman. The most likely arrangement would have been someone local who was contracted by the Postal Service to deliver the mail. The historical record, such as Lavina Eastlick's account, clearly indicates there was a mail carrier on the New Ulm to Sioux Falls route. These accounts also suggest that the mail carrier was known to the settlers along the way, including the settlers at Leavenworth and Shetek. This would indicate that the mail carrier was a regular on that route and could be anticipated at specific times and dates.

Not all the survivors of the Shetek attack, however, refer to a mail carrier in their accounts, most likely because they never encountered him in their flight. Alomina Hurd (and her two children), Lavina Eastlick (and her two children), and Tommy Ireland[35] were the seven people who were rescued or found by the mail carrier from Sioux Falls. Some mentioned the carrier and his name, "Spot." In her account, Mrs. Eastlick referred to him as the mail carrier, without naming him.[36] In her first account in Bryant's history, she indicated that she knew who he was. When the mail carrier first spoke to her in Dakota because he thought she was an Indian, Lavina writes, "I knew he was a Frenchman, so I talked to him in the same tongue."[37]

Aaron Myers who left Shetek before the events at Slaughter Slough said that the only name he knew for the mail carrier was Spot.[38]

---

[33] The federal census did not include the mythical towns of the 1857 territorial census. Cornwell is not included on the 1860 census, but the settlers around Lake Shetek are.

[34] See, for example, Kinsley, Maxine Schuurmans. 2010. *The Sioux City to Fort Randall Military Road 1856-1892*. Sioux Falls, SD: Pine Hill Press.

[35] Workman, p. 38, reference to Spot VanMeter

[36] Workman, p. 92: Workman said that Mrs. Eastlick knew the mail-carrier was Spot.

[37] Bryant & Murch, p. 356.

[38] Curie papers, archives of the Minnesota Historical Society; see also Workman, p. 62; Myers said it was Spot VanMeter

Mrs. Eastlick was the first picked up, near Buffalo Lake, on August 23 (Saturday) around noon. The second person rescued was Tommy Ireland, who was at Dutch Charley's cabin, when the mail carrier and Lavina arrived there in late afternoon on the 23rd. Ireland, although wounded several times, was well enough to keep pace with the mail wagon, led by the post man who walked, leading the horse. The third group, Alomina Hurd and her two children, were picked up around noon the next day, Sunday, August 24th, about five or so miles west of the Brown cabin east of Springfield. Merton and Johnnie were picked up shortly after, some two miles from the Brown cabin. Hurd, Ireland, and Eastlick all knew the postman from their own experience with him.

They describe the man as driving a sulky, a two-wheeled cart, pulled, likely, by a single horse. Today a sulky is used in horse or dog racing, but in the 19th century it was well adapted to transporting a few passengers or a light load, just what a mail man would use across the prairie. In addition to the front bench which would hold two persons, there may have been a box or platform on the back which could carry boxes or additional passengers. The postal regulations allowed a postman to carry up to two persons on his mail route.

Lavina Eastlick indicates that the mail carrier loaded her into the sulky and he walked, leading the horse. Tommy Ireland walked alongside and later when Mrs. Hurd and her children were picked up, they were also loaded into the sulky while the post man led the horse. The same thing happened to Johnnie and Merton. The sulky must have been quite full and a load for a horse to pull with two adults and four children, but it had only a couple of miles to go before they reached the Brown house around noon, where they stopped. After feeding his horse, the postman left the others and went alone to New Ulm that same night. He told them that he would send help from someone he knew, some seven miles further, probably in the Leavenworth area. If he did check on the person he knew in Leavenworth, he likely found an empty cabin because the residents of Leavenworth had by this time fled their homes or had been killed. The mail carrier probably arrived at New Ulm on Monday afternoon. The distance from the Brown house to New Ulm on the mail route was about 27 miles.

The post man returned on Tuesday (August 26) evening, but he stayed outside because he was uncertain as to who was in the cabin. The next morning he found the others and told them there was no help coming from New Ulm. He reported that New Ulm had been burned and there were some people walking the streets. He could not tell whether they were Dakota Indians or whites.[39] Not knowing whether the persons where friendlies or hostiles, he turned around and went back to the Brown cabin. Because the Mrs. Eastlick and Mrs. Hurd were fearful of remaining in the cabin where the Dakota could find them, the postman helped

---

[39] If he arrived in New Ulm on Monday, it isn't clear just whom he saw. New Ulm had been evacuated on Monday and by the time he arrived, the caravan would have been long gone. Capt. Joseph Anderson and his cavalry company reached New Ulm on the 26th (Tuesday), but finding no one, they went on to St. Peter. There could have been some New Ulm citizens who had returned. Company E of the 9th Minnesota Regiment under Capt. Jerome Dane arrived in New Ulm on Wednesday, the 27th.

the Eastlicks, Ireland, and the Hurds move out into the field to better hide themselves. He then said goodbye and told them he would send help from Sioux Falls. He left Wednesday morning and that is the last that is heard of the post man.

One of the factors in how the postman helped the refugees relates to the distance the postman traveled in a day. A wagon in the 18th century, such as a Conestoga or farm wagon, could travel about 30 miles in an 8 to 10 hour day.[40] Towns apparently were often some 30 miles distant from each other, which provided a distance for a farmer to get to a town in one day. New Ulm and Mankato are about that distance from each other and the evacuees of New Ulm reached Mankato in the evening after leaving New Ulm at 8:00 am. That was a caravan of some 200 wagons and 1500 persons.

A sulky, such as what the post man drove, probably traveled faster providing the land was relatively flat and there were few creeks or rivers to ford. A driver would still be limited, however, to the endurance of a horse and 10 hours with a good horse would be a reasonable time if the rider did not want to injure the horse; the distance could be between 35 and 45 miles a day. The New Ulm to Sioux Falls trail is about 170 miles long, depending on how much the route shown on the map differs from the actual trail.[41] It is about 35 miles from Sioux Falls to the Minnesota border, another 37 miles is near the Great Oasis, another 28 miles to Buffalo Lake, another 14 to Dutch Charley's cabin, another 29 miles to the Brown cabin, and a final 27 miles to New Ulm.

The postman left Sioux Falls in the morning (figuring backwards from the dates in the accounts), on Friday, August 22nd.[42] He stopped the night somewhere near or east of the small settlement of Pipestone. He continued on Saturday, August 23rd south of Lake Shetek, past Slaughter Slough (and noticed nothing?), and on to Buffalo Lake, arriving there around 2:00 in the afternoon. He picked up Lavina, and continued on another 15 miles to Dutch Charley's cabin. That would have been a long day, some 60 miles with the last 15 miles at a walk. Lavina and the postman did arrive in the evening. The next day (Sunday, August 24th), with Lavina in the sulky and Tommy Ireland and the post man walking, they started out.

Around 10:00 am, some 22 miles from Dutch Charley's cabin, they came upon Mrs. Hurd and her two children. That would mean they left Dutch Charley's quite early in the morning to travel 22 miles. That is possible, sunrise would come early, around 5:30 that day, and Mrs. Eastlick would certainly have been eager to get on the way because she knew Merton and Johnny were somewhere ahead of her. A couple miles later (10:30 am?), after picking up Mrs. Hurd and her

---

[40] Because there were many factors in how far someone could travel in a wagon (terrain, horse, load, type of wagon), there are few guides to such travel. The old favorite source, sort of the 19th century AAA road guide, was Marcy's book (Randolph B. Marcy. *The Prairie Traveler*. Bedford MA, First published in 1859 and reprinted by Applewood reprints). Marcy indicates that a Oregon Trail wagon would travel about 16-18 miles a day (p. 45).

[41] The distance today by highway is 167 miles and keeping within the speed limit, a driver can arrived in 3.5 hours.

[42] That is the date that Bryant and Murch, quoting Masters, give. p. 161.

children, they would have caught up to Merton and Johnnie. The eight refugees continued on and reached the Brown house at noon on Sunday. The last five miles undoubtedly included much talking, weeping, and rejoicing among the Hurds, the Eastlicks, and Tommy Ireland.

That Sunday night, the postman left the Brown cabin and made his way to New Ulm, arriving there Monday. He did not go into town, but turned around and came back to the Brown cabin on Tuesday, and left Wednesday for Sioux Falls. We don't know when he arrived back at Sioux Falls to find the town deserted. He may have traveled quickly, but cautiously, back and he was no longer encumbered with refugees, so he might have made it back in two or three days, arriving in Sioux Falls on Friday/Saturday, August 29/30. One would expect he was disappointed on finding the empty town. On August 28th the Territorial Governor, William Jayne, ordered that Sioux Falls be evacuated because of the attack on the Amidons and because of the news of the Dakota War in Minnesota. Most of the residents of Sioux Falls went to Yankton. The postman was therefore unable to find someone to go to the Brown cabin and he had no one to hear the story he could tell.

The survivor accounts, such as Lavina Eastlick's book, indicate that he then went on to Yankton; some suggest he went east to Dubuque, Iowa. In their history, Bryan and Murch, quoting Henry Master's account said

> When he [the mail-carrier] returned, the place was deserted. He procured some provisions here, and made his way to Vermilion, twenty eight miles below Yankton, on the Missouri River. He had left his horse between the Falls and Vermilion, entirely worn out, and unable to travel any further.[43]

Either destination was possible because both would have been occupied. There are also accounts of a mailman who was killed at this time between Sioux Falls and Yankton, but there are no details as to who this postman was.[44] The residents who fled Sioux Falls went to Yankton and some to Sioux City. Sioux City was a large town that was prepared to defend itself against attack.

The identity of this resolute post man has interested people since the story was first told. Lavina Eastlick (according to Workman) and Tommy Ireland refer to him as "Spot." Workman, based on what he heard from the survivors and apparently what he knew of the history of that area, concluded that this Spot was Spot VanMeter, whom Workman believed to have been a full or mixed blood Dakota

---

[43] Bryant & Murch (1864), quoting Masters, p. 162. There is an issue with this quote, however. Henry Masters, the author of the quotation, was elected President of the Council in the first Dakota Territorial Legislature in 1859. In that brief session, where the people of eastern Dakota Territory petitioned Congress for territorial status, Masters was elected (or nominated—there is disagreement) Governor of the Territory. He died a couple of days later. He could not have witnessed the event in the quote. Bryant and Murch do not provide the source of that quotation. It could have been a newspaper article about Masters, rather than by Masters. Bryant and Murch may also have gotten the author's name wrong. Henry Masters had a son, Harry (Henry, Jr.) Masters, in Yankton. Harry was alive and living in Yankton when the postman returned.

[44] See Armstrong, 1901, p. 36.

Indian. Mrs. Eastlick, however, referred to him as a Frenchman.[45] Workman indicates that Ireland, whom Workman interviewed, believed him to be a relative of Chief Sleepy Eyes, perhaps part French or part German and part Dakota. It also appears from the Workman papers that Ireland also knew him after the Dakota War.[46]

There is a brief biography of Arthur VanMeter in the South Dakota Historical Collections.[47] VanMeter came from Virginia (which cast doubts on Workman's and Ireland's description of him). He moved to Vermillion, Dakota Territory, as a young man (20) sometime in 1857/58. This is about the time Vermillion, which is on the Missouri River in southeastern South Dakota, was changing from a trading post to a town site. He built a cabin there and operated a rope ferry on the Vermillion River. He is listed in the 1860 census as Arthur C. VanMeter, 26, and in that household were Mary, 18, Viola, 1, and Ellen Angion, 8. His occupation was given as a ferryman born in Virginia; Mary, probably his wife, and the two children were mixed bloods, born in Dakota.

He also carried mail from Sioux City to Fort Randall.[48] There is an account of him being in Elk Point at the time of the Dakota War.[49] Elk Point is about 20 miles north of Sioux City and near Vermillion. The account appears to invent a conversation he had with some residents of Elk Point. VanMeter warns the residents that he heard that a settler had been killed on the James River and there was fighting around Vermillion. There is no specific date of this account and together with the uncertainty whether the account is accurate, it cannot be determined whether VanMeter could be in Elk Point after he returned from New Ulm.

Agnes Christina Laut, a Canadian historian and author of the early 20th century, and Doane Robinson, the South Dakota historian, claimed that Spot was not VanMeter, rather he was (August) Garzine.[50] Robinson said the mailman was German and Robinson in his correspondence with Myers said that Myers claimed the man was a Dutchman (the local term for German). In rejecting Workman's claim about VanMeter, Robinson further claimed that the VanMeters lived at Vermillion and were not in Minnesota during those years.

[45] Only in the version that Eastlick sent to Bryant and Murch does she continually refer to the mail-carrier as a Frenchman, and in that version she also spoke to him in French. In the later printings, she never names the mail-carrier nor does she refer to him as French. It is doubtful that Lavina Eastlick spoke French, given her background and ancestry. This may be a place where Eastlick was confused or misleading.

[46] Workman nd, 62-63

[47] State Department of History, compiler. *South Dakota Historical Collections*, Vol X. Pierre, SD: Hipple Printing, 1920, p. 535

[48] See Kinsley, pp 38, 85, 87

[49] State Department of History, compiler. *Collections of the South Dakota Historical Society*, Vol I. Pierre, SD: Hipple Printing, 1900, page 536

[50] Workman nd, 91

Robinson said there was no one with the name "Spot" VanMeter but there was a Spot (Samuel) Mortimer, and old frontiersman.[51] Partly because Mortimer came to Oakwood Lakes in 1869, Robinson also rejected Mortimer as the postman.

Agnes Laut said the mailman was August Garzine and Robinson concurred. But there is no indication of how Ms. Laut came to that conclusion. August Garzine (Garzin) is on the 1860 census in Vermillion. He is listed as a 30-year-old laborer who was born in France. He apparently came to Vermillion in 1859 and later, in 1862, became a member of Co. C, Dakota Militia.[52] Although Robinson suggests that Ms. Laut published her findings, an extensive search of her publications failed to identify that article or book. Although she was a prolific author, most of her work would be classified as history with a good dose of fiction. Nor does Robinson in his correspondence with Ms. Laut[53] give any reasons why he accepted Laut's conclusion, other than his belief in her scholarship. That wasn't good enough for Workman, however, and he still contended it was Spot VanMeter. Arthur VanMeter was living in Vermillion at the time and Workman said he also went by the name of "Spot."[54] Thus, Workman, considering the given name of "Spot" as essential in identifying the mailman, concluded the mail man must have been Spot Mortimer or Spot VanMeter.

Then there is Dr. W. W. Wilson who wrote to Workman in 1927 in a reply to a newspaper article on the Shetek attack. In his letters Wilson claimed to have been the post man. He said he was 82 years old and writing from Bovey, Minnesota. That would have made him 17 in 1862. He recalled picking up Merton and Johnny Eastlick and taking them to Fort Ridgely, but he did not recall picking anyone else up. Workman dismissed his story because of the inaccuracies and concluded Wilson was an imposter.[55]

Henry or Harry Masters (see above), whom Bryant and Murch quote for where the mail-carrier went after returning to Sioux Falls, may be an independent witness as to who this mail-carrier was. If the mail carrier went to Vermillion because that was his home, the mail carrier could be VanMeter.

[51] A historical marker on a lake area northwest of Brookings, South Dakota, provides the following information: "Samuel was a shoemaker who came here from New York. In 1869 he found his way to Oakwood Lakes which was a trappers paradise. Samuel built this cabin and lived here for the next 5 years. By 1874 his traplines were declining. So he built a sawmill and he played an important roll in providing lumber for many of houses and area businesses. After the death of his wife Samuel left here and moved to Yankton Dakota Territory where he married his next wife. They moved back to the cabin and lived there until 1886 at which time they sold the cabin and 1200 acres for $1,800." http://www.waymarking.com/waymarks/WMGHX_Ol_Spot_Mortimers_Cabin

[52] State Department of History, compiler. *South Dakota Historical Collections,* Vol X, Pierre SD: Hipple Printing, 1920, p. 422.,

[53] Robinson Collections Box 3362A, South Dakota Historical Society Archives

[54] Workman nd, 180

[55] It didn't help that Wilson claimed to be of English noble blood, had attended the Royal College in England, and had traveled through South America, Africa, China, and Palestine.

In summary, Robinson and Laut dismissed Mortimer and VanMeter, although both were in the Dakota Territory at the time and both may have had "Spot" as their first name or common name. Robinson and Ms. Laut asserted that August Garzine was the mailman.

On the other hand, Samuel Mortimer, whose friends called him Spot, was born in Missouri around 1835, which would have made him 27 in 1862. According to the census, in 1870 he was living in Fort Thompson, Dakota Territory and working as a wood cutter. We also know that a "Spot" VanMeter, 26, was living in Vermillion at this time and the mail carrier did return to Vermillion. The nationality of the mail carrier probably was not French, but some kind of mixed blood seems likely. None of the three surnames, Garzine, Mortimer, and VanMeter is distinctly French or German, two may have had given names or common names of "Spot," and all were definitely or probably in the area in 1862.

So, who was the postman? The reader is invited to draw her or his conclusion.

The Lake Shetek Settlement

The settlers at Shetek had built their cabins on the east side of the lake where game and wood were more abundant and there was more protection from the elements. (See Plate 10.) The nine inhabited cabins were arranged from north to outh. On the northern end of the lake were Aaron Myers (Meyers)[56] (37)[57] with wife Mary (36), and children Olive (12), Arthur (11), Fred (5), and Addie (1). Three-fourths of a mile south was the Hurd cabin. In that cabin were Phineas who was absent that day, his wife Alomina (26), William (3), and a baby of one. Also living in this cabin were William Jones, who was also absent that day, and John Voigt. A mile south, across Bloody Lake, was the Koch (Cook) cabin. Andrew with his wife Maria/Christina (26). Also living in the cabin was E.G. Koch (26), no relation. A mile south was the Ireland cabin with Thomas (49), wife Sophia, Rosana (9), Ellen (7), Sarah (5), and Juliane (3). A mile southwest was the Eastlick family, a family of seven: father John (39), mother Lavina (29), Merton (11), Frederick (4), Frank (10). Giles (8), and Johnnie (1). A half mile further down the lake was the Duley (Duly) cabin. William (43), his wife Laura (35), and their children William Jr. (10), Emma (8), Jefferson (6), Belle (5), and Francis (1) lived here. A mile south lived the Smith family, Henry and his wife, Sophia (37). A mile south of that was the Wright cabin. John Wright the father, was absent

---

[56] The names of the settlers had various spellings in the documents. Sometimes this appears to have been an attempt by others to anglicize a foreign name (Zierke to Sierke, Koch to Cook). Sometimes it appears to be a variant spelling (Myers to Meyers). Sometimes the settler actually preferred one spelling over the other (Duley to Duly). There are also variations in the spellings of the given name of a settler and sometimes even a different first name, particularly of the children. Tables 1, 2, and 3, provide several alternate names and spellings. This document uses what appeared to be the dominant spelling of a name.

[57] The ages of the settlers is given where it can be determined either because one of the documents includes the person's age at the time of the attack or because the birth date is given. There are variances in these dates for some of the settlers; even the Shetek monument has inaccurate ages. What is used here seems to be a consensus or it fits the circumstances of the person. Where ages are not given, none were available in the documents.

that day. His wife Julia (23), and their three children, Dora (6), George (4), and a baby were at home. Less than a mile south was the Everett cabin: husband William, wife Almina, and children Lillian (6), Willie (5), and Charley (2). An old map in the Workman[58] papers also indicates several other cabins or previous occupants of the current cabins. Two of these were trading posts, once occupied by three traders with the names of Jacques, Evans, and Jessup.

The man named Jacques, no first name given, settled in the Lake Shetek area in 1854 near or in the first trading post. In 1854 only Dakota Indians were in the area and Jacques both trapped and traded with the Dakota. In 1861 he left the Shetek area because he felt the Dakota were becoming too threatening. There is also a William Jacques (Jaques) who settled in Leavenworth Township (Brown County). He and his family are listed in the 1857, 1860, and 1865 censuses. This could be the same person.[59]

The other cabin or trading post is shown as the residence of Rhodes, another the home of Bently (Bentley), another the cabin of Charley Hatch, the brother of Almina Everett.[60] Rhodes, Bently, and Hatch are in the stories of Shetek, but their cabins are shown only in this one source. In a letter from Aaron Myers to Neil Currie.[61] Myers said there was a Mr. Rhodes and Macabee who were not settlers at Shetek, they had come there to avoid the draft The Workman map shows a Macabee cabin on Loon Island in Lake Shetek. Workman also mentions a Frank (Joe) LaBusch[62] who was a half-breed trapper in the area.

Depending on how the settlers are counted, there were 47[63], 45[64], or 50[65] persons at the lake on August 20, 1862. (See Tables 2-4 for a summary of the settlers grouped by their status after the attack, pages 28-29.)

---

58 Workman, Harper. 1924. Early History of Lake Shetek County. An unpublished typed manuscript. Shetek Collection, Brown County Museum, Brown County Historical Society, New Ulm, MN., 144ff. The Workman manuscript is available in a number of locations, including in microfilm at the Minnesota Historical Society.

59 The reference to Jacques, the trader at Lake Shetek, is found in "A Brief History of Murray County" by R.W. Terry, which appears to have been printed in the *Slayton Pioneer*, no date given.

60 Charley Hatch may have had his own cabin, but the accounts also have him living with his sister and brother-in-law, the Everetts.

61 Myers, Aaron. 1894. Letter to Neil Currie, November 20. Shetek Collection, Brown County Museum, Brown County Historical Society, New Ulm, MN.

62 This is one of the confusing names. Workman gives several spellings including LaFramboise, LaBasche, Laboshe, LaBush, LaFramboshe, Joe LaFramboise Jr. The map shows a cabin for a LaBosche on the west side of the lake. Other records frequently mention a Joseph LaFramboise, a well-known fur trader who helped to rescue the whites at Big Stone Lake [Bryant, Charles S. and Abel B. Murch. 2001. *Indian Massacre in Minnesota*. Cincinnati, OH: Rikey & Carroll, 1863. Repr., Scituate, MA: DSI Digital Reproduction (page references are to the reprint edition). p214]. A LaFramboise also is in the Shetek story. The records do not indicate whether these are all the same person.

63 Gray, John. 1975. The Santee Sioux and the Settlers at Lake Shetek. Montana, T*he Magazine of Western History,* Winter, 42-54, p 42

64 Heard, Isaac V.D. 1864. *History of the Sioux War and Massacres of 1862 and 1863*. New York: Harper & Brothers, p. 99

65 Dahlin, Curtis A. 2007. *Dakota Uprising Victims*. Edina: Beavers PondPress, p. 95

Also at the lake was a group of Santee Dakota Indians. The number is uncertain; some have estimated 30. Bryant[66] puts the number of Dakota at 20. Dahlin[67] lists their leaders as White Lodge (Wakagyaska),[68] Lean Grizzy Bear,[69] and Old Pawn. The Dakota rarely had a "leader" in the sense that white armies had, but some sources[70] indicated that Lean Bear was the leader. One of the Dakota camps was located on the south end of the lake near the Wright cabin. Oehler describes White Lodge and Lean Bear as Sisseton chiefs who had located their village 60 miles south of the reservation, which could have put them near Lake Shetek.[71] An article on a gathering of the survivors in 1895 gives the names of Chaska, Tizzie Tanka, Titonah, and Bad Ox.[72] Pawn, Old Pawn, or Across the River is often characterized as the villain in the events at Shetek.[73] Satterlee[74] was convinced that Pawn was actually Inkpaduta. By one account Old Pawn was 6'3" and "one of the worst looking Indians I ever saw."[75] Pawn was well known to the settlers and they believed him to be their friend. He had his camp near the Wright cabin. When the settlers fled to the Wright cabin, they found Old Pawn already there preparing to defend the Wright cabin from the other Dakota.[76]

[66] Bryant, Charles and Edward Neill. 1882. *History of the Minnesota Valley including Explorers and Pioneers of Minnesota and History of the Sioux Massacre.* Minneapolis: North Star., p. 215

[67] Dahlin, Curtis A. 2007. *Dakota Uprising Victims.* Edina: Beavers Pond Press, p. 95.

[68] White Lodge, after the death of Sleepy Eyes (Ishtabo) in c. 1860 became the leader of part of the band while a nephew took his uncle's name and was chief over the other portion. These two bands were in the Lake Benton area and participated in the attack on Shetek (1969. *Indian Chiefs of Southern Minnesota.* Comp. Thomas L. Hughes. Minneapolis, MN: Ross and Haines, p. 107). These bands were of the Sisseton tribe which did not, for the most part, participate in the 1862 War.

[69] Lean Grizzy Bear was often referred to as Lean Bear. He may have been the same Lean Bear that was a member of Red Iron's band. He is described by Buck [Buck, Daniel. 1965. *Indian Outbreaks.* Mankato: Unknown, 1904. Repr., Minneapolis: Ross & Haines (page references are to the reprint edition).p. 68] as "a large, resolute man, about thirty-five years of age, and had great influence in his nation." (See also Hughes, Thomas. 1969. *Indian Chiefs of Southern Minnesota.* Comp. Thomas L. Hughes. Minneapolis, MN: Ross and Haines., p. 98)

[70] Wall, Oscar Garrett. 1909. *Recollections of the Sioux Massacre.* Lake City, MN: The Printery, p. 162.

[71] Oehler, C. M. 1959, 1997. *The Great Sioux Uprising.* New York: Da Capo Press. p. 24

[72] *Minneapolis Tribune,* July 11, 1895.

[73] Lavina Eastlick describes him with those words. Eastlick, Lavina. *1864. Thrilling Incidents of the Indian War of 1862: Being a Personal Narrative of the Outrages and Horrors Witnessed by Mrs. L. Eastlick in Minnesota.* Lancaster, Wisconsin: Herald Book and Job Office. [This and all other quotations are taken from the most recent reprinting (2010) of the Eastlick booklet by the Murray County Historical Society. This reprinting has pagination. References are noted as Eastlick, 1864, page or preface.] p. 10.

[74] Satterlee, Marion. 2001. *Outbreak and Massacre by the Dakota Indians in Minnesota in 1862.* Ed. Don Heinrich Tolzmann. Westminster, MD: Heritage Books, p. 51.

[75] Workman, quoting Luther Ives, 1924, p. 87

[76] Bryant, Charles S. and Abel B. Murch. 2001. *Indian Massacre in Minnesota.* Cincinnati, OH: Rikey & Carroll, 1863. Repr., Scituate, MA: DSI Digital Reproduction (page references are to the reprint edition), p. 344.

Table 2: The Survivors at Shetek

Settler	Birth/Death	Note
Burns, John F	?	Walnut Grove
Burns, Daniel	?	Walnut Grove
Bently (Bentley), Edgar (John)	(1832-?)	
Duley, William	(1819-1898)	
Everett,William	(1831-1892) (1898)	
Eastlick, Mrs. John (Lavina)	(1833-1923)	
Eastlick, Merton	(1851-1875)	
Eastlick, Johnnie	(1861-1942)	
Hatch, Charles (Brother of Lillian Everett)	(1837-1907)	
Hurd, Baby (Christina/Charles?)	(1861-?)	
Hurd, Mrs. Phineas (Almina)	(1836-1922)	
Hurd, Phiniasia (Phineas)	(1833-1862?)	(absent/killed?)
Hurd, William Henry	(1859-?)	
Ireland, Thomas	(1812-1897)	
Jones, William (lived with Hurd family)		(absent/killed?)
Koch, E.G.	(1833-1919)	(absent)
Myers, Aaron	(1825-1906)	
Myers, Addie (Abbie, Eliza?)	(1861-?)	
Myers, Arthur	(1851-1907)	
Myers, Fred (Frederick)	(1857-1863)	
Myers, Olive (Eliza?)	(1854-)	
Myers, Mrs. Aaron (Mary)	(1826-1862)	
Myers, Louisa	(1850-1900)	(absent)
Rhodes (not a settler at Shetek) (A.A.?)	(1839-?)	
Smith, Henry Watson	(1820-?)	
Wright, John	(1835-?)	(absent)
Zierke, Charlie (Dutch) (Karl)	(1828-1865)	Cottonwd Cnt
Zierke, Christina (Schumacher)	(1826-	Cottonwd Cnt
Zierke, John (stepchild)	(1849-	Cottonwd Cnt
Zierke, Henry (stepchild)	(1852-	Cottonwd Cnt
Zierke, Elliza (Louisa) (stepchild)	(1856-	Cottonwd Cnt
Zierke, Mary	(1858-	Cottonwd Cnt
Zierke, Anne	(?)	Cottonwd Cnt

Table 3: Settlers Killed at Shetek or on the Shetek Trail

Name	Birth/Death	Where killed	Buried
Brown, (Hank, Sam, Old) Joseph	(1789-1862)	road to New Ulm	Springfield
Brown, Jonathan	(1825-1862)	road to New Ulm	Springfield
Brown, Horatia	(1830-1862)	road to New Ulm	Springfield
Duley, Belle (Isabella)	(1858-1862)	Slough	Shetek grave
Duley, William jr.	(1852-1862)	Slough	Shetek grave
Eastlick, Frank	(1852-1862?)	Slough	Unknown
Eastlick, Frederick	(1858-1862)	Slough	Shetek grave
Eastlick, Giles	(1854-1862)	Slough	Shetek grave
Eastlick, John	(1823-1862)	Slough	Shetek grave
Everett, Willie	(1857-1862)	Slough	Shetek grave
Everett, Charley	(1860-1862)	Slough	Shetek grave
Everett, Mrs. William (Almina Hatch)	(?-1862)	Slough	Shetek grave
Ireland, Julianne	(1859-1862)	Slough	Shetek grave
Ireland, Mrs.. Thomas (Sophia)	(?-1862	Slough	Shetek grave
Ireland, Sarah Jane	(1857-1862)	Slough	Shetek grave
Koch, Andrew	(1817-1862)	Koch cabin	unknown
Smith, Mrs.. Henry Watson (Julia/Sophia)	(1825-1862)	Slough	Shetek grave
Voigt (Voight), John	(?-1862)	Hurd cabin	Shetek grave
Wright, infant captured and killed	(?-1862)	Unknown	Unknown

Table 4: Taken Captive at Shetek

Settler	Birth/Death	Released	Captured
Koch, Mrs. Andrew (Maria/Christina?) Hockmuth	(1835?-1907)	Camp Release	slough
Ireland, Rosana (Rose, Roseann)	(1853-1936)	Pierre	slough
Ireland, Eillen (Ella, Ellen)	(1855-1946)	Pierre	slough
Duley, Mrs.. William (Laura)	(1827-?)	Pierre	slough
Duley, Jefferson (John?)	(1856-1937)	Pierre	slough
Duley, Francis (Candis)	(1862-1862)	died in captivity	slough
Duley, Emma	(1854-1927)	Pierre	slough
Everett, Ablillian (Lillian)	(1856-1923)	Pierre	slough
Wright, Mrs. John (Julia)	(1837-?)	Pierre	Slough
Wright, Dora (Eldora)	(1856-1865)	Pierre	Slough
Wright, George	(1858-?)	Camp Release	Slough

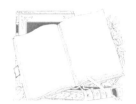

The Narrative Sources

The attack on the settlers at Lake Shetek where John Eastlick and three of his children were killed, in what at that time was called the Shetek Massacre, is fairly well know. The Dakota War was a major event and a subject for many written narratives that were shared with family, friends and the public.

Some of these accounts were published shortly after the Dakota War; some were published much later as reminiscences.

Bryant and Murch included 15 narratives in their 1864 history of the Dakota War: Jonathan Earle, Mrs. Helen Carrothers, Mrs. Justina Krieger, Justina Boelter, Mary Schwandt, Lavina Eastlick, Alomina Hurd, Duncan Kennedy, Anton Manderfeld, J. H. Adams, Nehemiah Miller, Gure Anderson, Ernestina Broberg, Valencia Reynolds, Mary Werley. Many of these stories were collected by the Reparations Commission which met in the spring of 1863 in St. Peter. As part of their claim for reparations for damages they suffered during the Dakota War, the settlers recounted what happened to them. Charles Bryant was part of that Commission and he recorded those stories. In the case of Justina Krieger, for example, Bryant asserts that the account was taken verbatim from the German translator when she appeared before the Commission. Sometimes the stories were published either before or after the testimony given to the Commission. Alomina Hurd, also a Shetek survivor, had her account published in the *Davenport* [Iowa] *Gazette* in the spring of 1863.

The reminiscences written years later included Jannette DeCamp,[77] Nancy McClure,[78] Mary Schwandt,[79] Urania White,[80] and John Humphrey.[81] There were also at least two survivors who published books or booklets describing their experiences. Both Sarah Wakefield and Lavina Eastlick published their accounts in 1863/1864.

The reasons these authors had for sharing their accounts varied somewhat. (Those who gave their accounts as part of their testimony to the Reparations Commission obviously did so as evidence for their claims.) Bryant gave this reason for publishing the accounts in his history: "to present, for the benefit of

[77] DeCamp, J. E. 1894. Sioux Outbreak of 1862: Mrs.. J. E. DeCamp's Narrative of her Captivity. In *Collections of the Minnesota Historical Society Vol 6,* Ed. The Society. St. Paul: Pioneer Press.

[78] McClure, Nancy. 1894. The Story of Nancy McClure. In *Minnesota Historical Society Collection Vol IV.* Ed. The Society. St. Paul, MN: Minnesota Historical Society.

[79] Schwandt, Mary. 1894. The Story of Mary Schwandt. In *Collections of the Minnesota Historical Society Vol 6,* Ed. The Society, 461-474. St. Paul, MN: Pioneer Press.

[80] White, N. D. 1901. Captivity Among the Sioux, August 19 to September 26, 1862. In *Collections of the Minnesota Historical Society, Vol. IX,* Ed. Minnesota Historical Society, 404-434. St. Paul, MN: Minnesota Historical Society.

[81] Humphrey, John Amos. 1915. Boyhood Remembrances of Life Among the Dakotas and the Massacre of 1862. In *Collections of the Minnesota Historical Society Vol XV,* Ed. The Society, 337-448. St. Paul, MN: Minnesota Historical Society.

the present and future generations, the astounding truths connected with this bloody drama in our history."[82] Sarah Wakefield wrote "for the special benefit of my children as they were so young at the time they were in captivity, that, in case of any death, they would, by recourse to this, be enabled to recall to memory the particulars…"[83] Sarah included two other reasons for writing: [to show] "what I suffered, and what I was spared from suffering, by a few Friendly or Christian Indians, " and "to vindicate myself, as I have been grievously abused by many, who are ignorant of the particulars of my captivity and release by the Indians." The second and third reasons relate to her beliefs about the Military Commission trials and how they dealt with her Dakota captors. Lavina Eastlick wrote "that people living at this distance from the scene of those atrocities[84] can arrive at any just and adequate conception of the fiendishness of the Indian character, or the extremities of pain, terror, and distress endured by the victims"[85]

Although there are differences among these "reasons," particularly in the Eastlick preface, there is a common element—to publish "a plain, unvarnished statement of all the facts." This was the catchphrase of Joe Friday—"just the facts, ma'm." None of the authors of the narratives was a professional writer. Wakefield apologizes for her amateur writing skills. She also dismissed the notion that she was writing for the money her books would earn. They all believed that their goal was to tell the story of what happened to them in an objective, truthful manner.

The Eastlick Book

But none of these narratives are "just the facts"; any narrative selects certain facts and ignores others, any narrative uses words that add a subjective element in the description and elaboration of those facts, and any narrative has the author's values and biases as its subtext. Sarah Wakefield wanted to expose the conspiracy, bias, and blatant incompetence of the Military Commission that tried and convicted Chaska. Mary Schwandt wrote two narratives, one antagonistic to the Dakota who captured her and another more favorable and sympathetic to them. Lavina wrote, perhaps unconsciously, as a way to ennoble her suffering and loss.

Although Lavina Eastlick obviously retained a strong belief in the "fiendishness" of the Dakota which colored her narrative, she probably did not substantially alter the events at Shetek. There were other survivors (who also probably shared those racial views in some degree) who gave accounts of Shetek.

---

[82] Bryant & Murch, 2001 (1863), Preface, iii

[83] Wakefield, Sarah F. (1863) *Six Weeks in the Sioux Tepees,* 2004 printing by Globe Pequot Press. Originally published: Minneapolis: Atlas Print. Co., Preface vii.

[84] She was writing this in Wisconsin.

[85] Eastlick, 1864, Preface.

Several wrote under their own names including Aaron Myers/Meyers,[86] Almina Hurd,[87] Maria Koch,[88] Charley Hatch,[89] William Duley.[90] The Workman Papers also have numerous letters, transcripts of conversations, and other documents on the Shetek incident. The general outline of the initial attack, the flight of the settlers to the Wright cabin, the panicked drive to Slaughter Slough, the killings and captures, and the journey of the survivors is fairly well established and these accounts are consistent with each other. Lavina Eastlick's booklet is the most comprehensive of the narratives.

These multiple accounts from different witnesses can also be used to examine some oral accounts of what happened at Shetek. One of these is the belief that there were two bands of Dakota. The first band drove the settlers to the Wright cabin. After negotiations, this Dakota band allowed the settlers to leave the cabin and go to New Ulm. On the way, a second band attacked the settlers. They were the ones who killed and took captive the settlers. A second oral account describes the settlers being released from the Wright cabin. The Dakota followed them because they wanted the horses, but they had no intent to harm the settlers. When one of the settlers shot Lean Bear, everyone started shooting and some of the settlers were killed and others taken prisoner. Neither of the accounts is in written form. The settler accounts, in some readings, might suggest either of these scenarios; the reader is invited to make her or his own judgment.

The development of the Eastlick narrative is fairly well documented in both Lavina's descriptions and in the publication history of the book. In her appendix to a later version of her booklet, she says she wrote the manuscript during the winter of 1863/64 and her preface is dated April 1, 1864. Bryant and Murch published their history in 1864 with the preface of that book by Bryant dated as November 1863. Lavina must have sent her manuscript to Bryant shortly after finishing it in April 1864. At that time she also included a letter giving a brief autobiography. This is where the misspellings of her name were included.[91]

Lavina Eastlick also told her story frequently in 1862 and 1863 even before she wrote it down. She spent five weeks in a Mankato hospital where she shared stories with William Everett and Charlie Hatch, both of whom were also hospitalized. She went to St. Paul to obtain a pass to go to Wisconsin and Governor

[86] Aaron Myers. 1900, 1906. Reminiscence and Biographical Data. Typed manuscript. Shetek Collection, Brown County Museum, Brown County Historical Society, New Ulm, MN.; The New Ulm Massacre by A. Myers. A Trader Relates Personal Experiences Immediately Prior to That Fiendish Human Butchery. Manuscript. Brown County Historical Society Archives This may have been an article in the Garrison S.D. newspaper published in the late 1800s.

[87] Bryant & Murch 2001 (1863), 367-375. See also French, John C. *The Heroine of Lake Shetek in Minnesota*, Altoona, PA: Times Tribune Press, 1923.

[88] Maria (Christina) Koch: *Winona Daily Republican*, October 22, 1862.

[89] Narrative of Charles D. Hatch's Experiences in the Indian War in Minnesota in 1862. Manuscript dated 1895, Brown County Historical Society Archives. See also Story of Indian Massacre Told by a Survivor, *Minneapolis Tribune*, August 18, 1912, also *Martin County Independent*, April 22, 1897.

[90] *Murray County Pioneer* April 12, 1888; also part of the unpublished Murray County History.

[91] Bryant and Murch, 2001 (1863), p. 365

Ramsey heard her story and convinced her and Merton and Johnny to pose for a photograph. On the stage from St. Paul to Rochester she met and told her story to John Stevens, a house painter, who later painted a panorama showing scenes from Shetek. At Rochester she met with Mrs. Andrew Koch who had been taken captive at Shetek and later freed at Camp Release. Lavina thus had another opportunity to tell her story and hear other information from Mrs. Koch about the captivity of the Shetek survivors. In St. Charles she spoke with Aaron Myers and they also traded stories about Shetek. By the time she got to her brother's home in Ellenboro, Wisconsin, she knew the story of Shetek well, both from her perspective and from the perspective of others. Her brother Leicester Day lived in Ellenboro and her older sister Diana Day Cooley lived nearby in Platteville. She stayed with her brother when she wrote her account. But before she wrote, she also told her story to J. C. Cover, the editor of the *Grant County Herald* in Lancaster (which later published the booklet). She said her story was told "in a very poor way…" because of the "many times [she] had previously related it." Nevertheless, the *Herald* published this account on December 2, 1862. This would be the first publication. (See Appendix B). There would be at least five more printings of the book.

After spending the summer of 1863 with her parents (Giles Day Jr. and Hannah), in Ohio, she returned to Ellenboro in the fall and wrote out the full account. It was published by the Herald Book and Job Office in Lancaster, Wisconsin. It was a booklet with a green paper cover and a format (8" x 5 ½") of 32 pages in 9 point type. The book must have sold well because she bought a team of horses, moved back to Minnesota, and bought some land in Mankato in 1866. She had a second printing of the book in 1864 by the Atlas Steam Press Co. in Minneapolis. The booklet was the same size and with slightly larger type it now ran to 37 pages. The title remained the same: *Thrilling Incidents of the Indian War of 1862: Being a Personal Narrative of the Outrages and Horrors Witnessed by Mrs. L. Eastlick in Minnesota*. These two first publications had an additional paragraph in the preface. In this paragraph she gave another reason for writing the narrative: "My object in publishing my story is two fold: I wish to inform the public as to the extent of the wrongs inflected upon the innocent Minnesotans, and I also hope and expect to realize from the proceeds of its sale sufficient pecuniary aid to enable me to return from my temporary home in Grant County, Wisconsin, to my desolate home in Minnesota—to the region where I left the bodies of my husband and three children, on the bloody sod where they fell."

Some 25 years later there was a third reprinting of the booklet. This was done by the Free Press Printing Co in Mankato in 1900 (See Fig. 2). The booklet remained the same size, now with a brown cover and 37 pages. This 1900 printing includes the Appendix that Lavina added to bring the story of her life up to 1890. In this Appendix she told how she wrote the account, her move to Mankato and her farm, her marriage to Solomon Pettibone, the birth of Laura, the death of Merton, and the marriage of Johnnie. This appendix was included in all subsequent printings. In the copy at the Blue Earth County Historical Society, she also wrote her signature. (See Fig 3.)

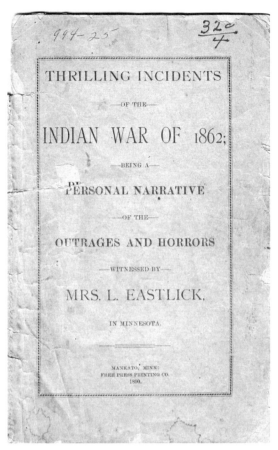

Fig. 2: Cover 1900 Printing

Then sometime in the first part of the 20th century a new printing came out in mimeograph form.[92] This was published by Lavina's daughter-in-law Margaret Eastlick, the wife of Johnnie, who arranged to have the narrative retyped on a stencil for mimeographing. Even more confusing, it duplicated the title page giving the date as 1900 and the printer as the Free Press in Mankato. This printing could have been done after Lavina died in 1923 and obviously before Margaret died in 1931, but that seems unlikely. In this mimeograph reprint there is an endnote assuring the reader that this is "an exact copy of the original printing" and that the mimeographing had been done by Margaret Eastlick "for the express purpose of preserving same for members of the Eastlick family." One copy of this same mimeograph has the date of December 9, 1946, which would be after Margaret's death. Another copy of this printing has the name "Harry Eastlick" written in a childish hand on the inside cover of the printing. (See Fig. 4.) Harry or Henry, was Margaret and Johnnie's son who was born in 1890. This would suggest a date of the early 1900s. Whatever the reason or whenever it was printed, if Harry was reading it, the printing was meeting its goal.

The fourth printing was apparently made for the 100th anniversary of the Dakota War. Again, it was 8 by 5½ with a paper cover. It included paintings from the Stephens panorama—a particularly lurid one was featured on the front cover—and it had larger type, but it still had 34 pages. It included the appendix and in place of the authentication paragraph that Margaret Eastlick included, the booklet had several notarized affidavits that attested to the truth of the narrative. It also include photographs of Lavina, Laura, Donald (Laura's son), John Stevens the artist, the Shetek monument, and Ross Irish, who was identified as a nephew of Lavina and the supplier of the documents and photographs. This printing also included a disclaimer that attempted to put the narrative in the context of the injustices that had been done to the Dakota people that prompted them to attack the settlers. This disclaimer may have been written by the Minnesota Historical Society, which is listed as the publisher. The date "1962" is penciled in the MHS archive copy.

---

[92] The mimeograph as a means of printing multiple copies came into widespread use around 1900. A commercial version had been invented earlier by David Gestetner in 1891. Margaret Eastlick might have had one available in Monticello where she was living at that time (1910). It would not have been possible for her to produce a mimeographed printing in 1890. She probably engaged someone in the Monticello area to type the stencil, first removing the carbon ribbon on the typewriter. Then she could have taken it to a newspaper or other printer who had a mimeograph. But this required that the machine was available in some towns like Monticello, or earlier, in Mankato.

The fifth and final reprinting appears to be an ongoing, undated publication, with pagination. The pictures and the affidavits remain, in addition to a letter from John T. Eastlick, Lavina's grandson. The lurid cover and the other pictures from the Stevens's Panorama were removed. The disclaimer remains, but there is no publisher or date indicated. A more recent printing (2010) by the Murray County Historical Society includes the date and the Society as the publisher.

Fig. 3: Eastlick signature on 1900 edition.

Despite the many printings, the story remained the same as it was first published in 1864. There are a few typos that were corrected, and some that were introduced in the various printings. For example, the 1864 printing had a "gentleman" giving Lavina a ticket to "Otomy" which was fifty miles from Mankato. In 1890 "Otomy" had become Owatonna, but in the 1946(?) printing the sentence disappeared. In the 1864 printings Lavina described an argument she had with he man who had agreed to file her reparations claim in return for a percentage of the amount. Lavina named him, Buck, but she refused to hire him because she felt his charges were exorbitant. In the 1890 edition, Mr. Buck's name had disappeared and an ellipse took its place. The name never appeared in any subsequent edition; either the name was in error in previous versions or Lavina didn't want any more hassles from him.

But, it is somewhat remarkable that in three printings during her life, Lavina did not change anything in her narrative. She must have felt that she got it right the first time.

There are occasionally one-book authors who put their life into that one book. Margaret Mitchell was a one-book author with *Gone With the Wind*. Ken Kesey was essentially a one-book author with *One Flew Over the Cuckoo's Nest*. Often one-book authors base the one book on personal experiences. Harper Lee (*To Kill and Mockingbird*) and J.D. Salenger (*The Catcher in the Rye*) put themselves into their books and there was nothing left to say in another book. While there are wide differences among Kesey, Mitchell, Lee, Salinger, and Eastlick, all of them had an intense personal involvement in what they wrote. Mitchell listened to stories of the Civil War growing up in Atlanta and Kesey worked in a mental hospital. Harper Lee lived her story and Salinger probably reflected on his own life experience. Their personal experiences, which were the backgrounds of the book, ensured that the book was, in a sense, them. Kesey, Lee, Salinger, and Mitchell became famous people because of that book, and they lived, as did Lavina, off the proceeds of that one book.

Lavina loved her children and she doted on her grandchildren. But that book she wrote was her. In that book she expressed her strong Christian beliefs, she justified her anger at those who killed her family, she excused her feelings about people who would cheat her, she proudly emphasized her humility and poverty.

Fig. 4: Harry Eastlick's Copy of "Thrilling Incidents..."

She marketed her book, sometimes at the expense of her family. She made sure that the book remained in print, and available for purchase during her lifetime. Laura, her daughter, knew the importance of that book. Laura managed to add to the book a note of authenticity from the provincial government of Alberta. After her mother died, Laura kept a copy of the book and loaned it out, but made certain it was returned to her.

The book actually outlived Lavina. It has remained available for 150 years, but it was never printed and marketed by a major publisher—except briefly by the Minnesota Historical Society who rather quickly dropped it after one printing. Individuals like John Eastlick's wife or Laura kept the book in print, perhaps they believed that as long as the book was available, Lavina would in a sense live on. Murray County Historical Society, the current publisher, says the book still sells well. Lavina would be the first to say that if you want to know Lavina, read her book.

Other Accounts

Early histories such as Bryant & Neill[93] and McConkey[94] include accounts of Shetek. Satterlee[95] also includes a brief account. Charlie Hatch and William Everett told their story to the *Mankato Independent* on August 29th.[96] They did not know at that time what had happened to some of the others, including Mrs. Eastlick, but the account they gave of the events leading up to the attack at Slaughter Slough is substantially the same as Lavina's account. Unlike the recollections of the other survivors of the 1862 War, Mrs. Eastlick's account was contemporary to the events and it must have been widely known at the time to be included in those early histories.

Late in the 19th century, Harper Workman, a medical doctor in Sleepy Eye, set himself the task of reconstructing the events at Shetek some 30 years after the event.[97] He contacted the survivors and sent to them a set of questions on events

---

[93] Bryant, Charles and Edward Neill. 1882. *History of the Minnesota Valley including Explorers and Pioneers of Minnesota and History of the Sioux Massacre.* Minneapolis: North Star.

[94] First published in 1863 McConkey, Harriet Bishop. 1864. *Dakota War Whoop.* St. Paul: Wm. J. Mosses Press.

[95] Satterlee, Marian. 1925 (2001). *Outbreak and Massacre by the Dakota Indians in Minnesota In 1862.* Ed. Don Heinrich Tolzmann. Westminister, MY: Heritage Books.

[96] Reprinted in the *St. Paul Pioneer and Democrat*, September 3, 1862. After this account, William Everett refused to talk about Shetek.

[97] Workman, 1924. Workman in the preface to his manuscript says that he first became interested in the Shetek event in the early 1880s when he was in Sleepy Eye. He never intended his manu-

leading up to the attack and the killings. He was quite successful, and many of the survivors, some of whom were children at the time, provided him with lengthy responses. In 1894 he and Neil Currie and the survivors, Tommy Ireland, Aaron Myers, Charlie Hatch, Lavina Eastlick and Johnnie (but not Laura), went out to Lake Shetek and found the locations of the cabins, often identifying the cabins by a depression in the ground. The survivors and Workman walked through the places where the events occurred.[98] Neil Currie (1842-1921) also compiled information on the victims of Lake Shetek and personal testimony of the survivors in 1894. Some of the compilations are duplicates of what Workman gathered and others are letters from the survivors. His material was privately published.[99]

Several area newspapers, at the time of the anniversaries of the Shetek Attack, printed special editions containing accounts and sometimes new interviews with the survivors. These accounts often included information on the lives and deaths of the survivors after the attack. The *Tracy Headlight Herald* did such an edition in 1932.[100] H. J. Hibschman in 1901 published an account of the events at Shetek. Much of his information came from a newspaper sketch published in 1887 which he obtained from Neil Currie.[101] At least two historical novels were also written.[102]

There are also personal papers from Aaron Myers, Charles Hatch, William Duley, and others, correspondence, official reports in the archives of a number of institutions, including the Minnesota Historical Society. Second hand accounts of the Shetek Attack include writers such as Carley, Dahlin, and Folwell. At least one DVD video has also been produced.[103]

There are rumors that at least two undiscovered manuscripts exist. One is by William Duley, a survivor of the attack. Its whereabouts is unknown and seems unlikely to surface at this late date.[104] The second missing source is a more recent

---

script would be published; rather he wrote it for his son so that he "might know something of the section in which he was born and of the sufferings and history of the first settlers." Preface

[98] See page 68.

[99] Currie, Neil. 1894, 1946. Information on Victims of the Lake Shetek Massacre Obtained by Correspondence and Personal Testimony. Typewritten manuscript.

[100] See also Silvernale, John A. 1970 (3rd printing). In Commemoration of the Sioux Uprising August 20, 1862. Slayton, MN: Murray County Historical Society.

[101] Hibschman, H. J. 1901. The Shetek Pioneers and the Indians. Typed manuscript. Shetek Collection, Brown County Museum, Brown County Historical Society, New Ulm, MN.).

[102] Sneve, Virginia Driving Hawk. 1974. *Betrayed*. New York: Holiday House. Smith, Aaron Michael. *Crimson Runs the Prairie*. Kearney, Nebraska, Morris Publishing 2010. In a brief moment of charming honesty by the authors, Sneve includes this line in the preface: "The Author was not confined by bare historic facts and used her imagination to develop characters, dialogue, and situations," and Smith confesses, "Historical purists could take exception to some details and characters as I have portrayed them here." Both authors are very accurate in these statements.

[103] *Return to Shetek: The Courage of the Fool Soldiers*. 2007. DVD`. Produced by Barbara Britain. DVD, 90 minutes. Personal.

[104] A Duley typewritten manuscript in the Murray County Museum was published in the *Murray County Pioneer* on April 12, 1888 and became part of the unpublished History of Murray County. This is not the missing Duley manuscript. In point of fact, there may not even be a Duley manuscript. Duley was a complex person, claiming things that he had done (such as

account, apparently written in the late 1960s/70s by Eric Johansson. At the time he was researching at Shetek and writing his intended book, *Shetek*. Johannson was a professor of medieval history in Kansas City, KS. The book, 400 pages long, was never published. Johansson had apparently found unknown source material for the events at Shetek and he found that some existing accounts were inaccurate. Some content of the book, such as the time line and location of the bodies along Slaughter Slough were used in newspaper articles. Johannson died some years ago and there is no trace of the manuscript itself. Some residents of the Shetek area read parts of Johannson's manuscript. They conclude, based on what he wrote and answers he gave to questions about his sources, that Johannson had found no new sources and much of the manuscript was based on his own assumptions and inventions.

Finally, there is the unpublished *History of Murray County from 1833 to 1950*. Pieces of it were published by Robert Forrest and J. D. Weber and are in the Murray County Historical Society archives.

Yes, these narratives are all from the side of the settlers; there were a few narratives from the Dakota people. The Dakota narratives that exist were mostly written by the Dakota who did not join in the fighting or killing. Snana, who rescued Mary Schwandt,[105] and Big Eagle[106] are two published Dakota accounts. Anderson and Woolworth[107] have also published a compilation of the narratives of the Dakota and mixed-bloods who lived during the Dakota War. There is also a rich oral tradition that includes stories that have never been published.[108] There are no known Dakota accounts, however, that relate directly to the events at Shetek.

---

building the scaffold on which the 38 Dakota were executed), making himself appear more noble than he was (descriptions of his injuries), and forcing himself on others so as to obtain an army pension when he never served in the army. When he describes his (missing) manuscript in the *Pioneer* he says it is "a historical skitch [sic] of the deeds and depredations of the Sioux outbreak which would make a book of about 100 pages which would contain nothing but solid facts. I think that there is money in such a book. I have been strongly impressed in my mind to take the lecture field myself, my wife and myself to travail [sic] with such certificates as we can procure. I think good money could be made by going east through the winter season. I being a prety [sic] good talker in public; perhaps we might form a junction and join in an enterprise of that kind and make it a profitable moove [sic]." Duley's reasons for writing sort of imply that the manuscript, if it does indeed exist, may be slanted for the aggrandizing of William Duley.

[105]   MHS Collections v. 9, 427-430,1901,St. Paul

[106]   MHS Collections v. 6, 382-400, 1894 St. Paul Pioneer Press

[107]   Anderson, Gary Clayton and Alan R. Woolworth. 1988. *Through Dakota Eyes: Narrative Accounts of the Minnesota Indian War of 1862*. St. Paul, MN: Minnesota Historical Society.

[108] American Indian Research Project, Oral History Center, University of South Dakota, Vermillion, SD which contains transcripts relating to the events of the Dakota War.

IV

The Attack on Shetek

The Prelude

Lake Shetek before the US-Dakota War appears to have been a peaceful settlement except for one unfortunate incident which made the point that this was still a frontier settlement. In 1860, two desperadoes came to Lake Shetek. Bill Clark, reportedly from Henderson or Shakopee, and Charlie Waubau (Wauban), said to be from New Ulm, fled from a robbery they had committed in St. Peter and came to Shetek, with or without the loot. The two disagreed over the division of the plunder (which they may have hidden before they arrived at Shetek). They came to Andrew Koch's house to continue the argument. John Wright, who was also sometimes described as a shady character, was there and he told Charlie Waubau to shoot Clark, which Waubau proceeded to do. Koch didn't want a dead body in his cabin so he told them to remove the body which they buried near the lake. Henry Smith, apparently also on the scene, took Waubau to Mankato to be tried. Waubau claimed self-defense because Clark had threatened to bring the Indians to kill all the settlers at Shetek. The jury acquitted Waubau after the witnesses supported his claim of being threatened. Waubau never returned to Lake Shetek and he apparently joined the army of Sibley or Sully in pursuit of the Dakota after the Conflict. There was a rumor that the stolen money had been buried near Charley Zierke's cabin on Dutch Charley's Creek. People were still looking for the loot in the early part of the 20th century, although the Workman papers indicate that a box of gold coins was found buried near Dutch Charley's cabin not long after the attack.

Other than this unpleasant incident, life at Shetek must have been quiet and pleasant. Most of the settlers were in similar circumstances—young families with children who felt they could live and prosper in this inviting lake region.

In November 1861 John and Lavina with their five boys came to Shetek and settled on 80 acres in the Northwest quarter of section 5, Township 107, Range 40. His home was on the shore of Lake Shetek and in back of the house was Hanover Slough. He and his family occupied one of the old fur trading-posts that had been abandoned. He reroofed it with sod which lasted until the spring rains in 1862 when he then started building a cabin. The cabin was never finished. The Dakota Indians named him "Friend Big Head," a complimentary name. Charlie Ireland, his former neighbor in Ohio, came at the same time (or 1859 or 1860, the dates vary) and settled on the other side of the section with his wife and four daughters.

One gets a sense of anticipation and a feeling of safety in Lavina Eastlick's account of how she and her husband and children found their way to Lake Shetek.

I felt a little fear of going there (Lake Shetek), knowing that there were a great many Indians in that and the adjoining counties; still, I was willing to accompany my husband wherever he thought he could best provide for his family. We started on our journey in the fall, taking nothing with us but our clothing, bedding, cattle, etc. … My husband chose to settle by a small lake, called Lake Shetek, where we arrived on the 5th of November. … My husband chose a beautiful spot for our home, situated about midway between the two ends of the lake. In the spring of 1862, he built a house and put in crops, and we began to feel quite happy and contented in our new home. I no longer felt any fear of the Indians; quite a number of them had lived by the lake all winter, and had been accustomed to come to our home almost every day.

The families at Shetek had celebrated the fourth of July in 1862 with a picnic by the lake, the Dakota seemed friendly, the crops looked good, their log cabins were simple but far better than sod houses; life was looking up on that warm August of 1862.

Living with the Eastlicks was Edwin Rhodes.[109] Rhodes was a trapper, age 25, unmarried, and a friend of the Eastlicks. Aaron Myers[110] claimed that Rhodes had come to Shetek to avoid the draft (Plate 10 shows the location of the settler cabins around Lake Shetek.)

The US-Dakota War Begins

The US-Dakota War began on Monday, August 18th with an attack on the Lower Sioux Agency by a group of Mdewakanton and Wakepute Dakota led by Little Crow. The agency buildings were burned, a number of women and children were taken captive, some traders and clerks were killed, and Capt. Marsh and his men from Fort Ridgely were ambushed at the Minnesota River ferry below the Agency. The refugees from these attacks fled east and north; the settlers of Lake Shetek, 50 miles to the southwest, were unaware of these events. On Tuesday, New Ulm was attacked for the first time and settlers were killed at Sacred Heart Creek, but, again, the settlers at Lake Shetek remain unaware of the events to the north and east, although Lavina in her account, and perhaps with hindsight, described clues she got from her husband that there was danger.

Although the Dakota had a leader, Little Crow, that did not mean that the Dakota had a carefully planned strategy for the War, other than driving the whites from Minnesota. Nor did it mean that the Dakota all acted in concert or even that all the Dakota concurred in the decision to attack the settlers. The

---

[109] Bryant, Charles and Edward Neill. 1882. p. 646 lists an Edwin Rhodes who was mustered into the 6th Infantry, Company E at Fort Snelling on October 10, 1862 and who deserted on January 20, 1863. This fits the information in the Workman manuscript which has Rhodes enlisting and soon deserting. The dates also fit because they follow the killings at Shetek and we know Rhodes escaped. See also Oehler 1959, 116.

[110] Myers, Aaron. 1894. Letter to Neil Currie, November 20. Shetek Collection, Brown County Museum, Brown County Historical Society, New Ulm, MN.

upper tribes, the Sisseton and Wahpeton, generally did not join in the attacks. In fact, the upper tribes warned and protected some of the settlers and the missionaries and storekeepers at the Upper Agency. The attacks on the settlers in southern Minnesota were spontaneous and random. Small groups of Dakota roamed around the country attacking settlers and looting as they found opportunity. Later in the War, Little Crow did devise a strategy of a pincher movement around Sibley at Fort Ridgely, but during the first week, attacks were generally unplanned and settlers died because they were in the wrong place.

This was likely the case at Lake Shetek. White Lodge and Lean (Grizzly) Bear, both Sisseton chiefs who chose to locate south of the reservation, had their camps near the edge of the Dakota Territory, some thirty-five miles from Shetek. Hubbard[111] has Lean Bear's camp near Lake Benton. Lean Bear took over part of Sleepy Eyes' band. Sometimes an account will indicate that Sleepy Eyes was part of the group that attacked Shetek. Such a reference could mean Lean Bear's band. There was another small Sisseton band lead by Limping Devil (or Thunder Face) which had their camp near Shetek. Limping Devil could be Old Pawn and the group located near Shetek. When White Lodge and Lean Bear heard of the attack on the Lower Agency and New Ulm, they sent a message to Little Crow, offering their help—unlike other Sisseton chiefs such as Red Iron. Little Crow asked them to participate in the Friday attack on Fort Ridgely.[112]

Lean Bear, White Lodge, and Limping Devil are referred to in an article in the *St. Paul Daily Press* (August 28, 1862). In this article, John Otherday, who rescued the missionaries from the Upper Agency, describes a council held by the two upper Dakota tribes, the Sissetons and the Wahpetons. On Monday, August 18th, the news of the attack on the Lower Agency reached the Upper Agency tribes. A council was called by the chiefs of the Sisseton and Wahpetons to determine what they should do—remain neutral or join the Lower Agency tribes in attacking the whites. John Otherday advised caution and peace as did some of the chiefs. There were, however, four chiefs or leaders who argued for war against the whites. These were Lean Bear, White Lodge, Limping Devil (White Lodge's father), and Blue Face. Either Limping Devil or Blue Face could have been Old Pawn. After the council, the majority of the Upper Agency tribes remained peaceful and eventually helped free the captives at Camp Release. The four chiefs, White Lodge, Lean Bear, Limping Devil and Blue Face, who were all Sissetons, left the council and began attacking white settlements, one of which was Shetek.

Pawn's band around Lake Shetek thus knew what their fellow tribesmen were doing at the Lower Agency and New Ulm and that a war had begun between the Indians and the whites. The Dakota at Shetek would have been unlikely to begin a conflict if they had not known what was happening to the north and east.

But at this point in time, it is difficult to know just what the Shetek Dakota set out to do on that Wednesday. These Dakota certainly shared the resentment over

---

[111] Hubbard, Lucius F. and Return I. Holcombe. 1908. *Minnesota in Three Centuries*, Vol 3. Mankato, MN: Publishing Society of Minnesota, p. 271

[112] Oehler, C. M. 1959, 1997. T*he Great Sioux Uprising*. New York: Da Capo Press, p. 105

the treaties that took their land, the lateness of the annuities, the perfidy of many traders who stole from them, and the growing fear that their culture and way of life was slipping away because of the settlers and the government. But why attack settlers, poor whites and their families trying to scratch out a living on the Minnesota prairie?

First, the Dakota didn't make careful distinctions among different groups of whites. There were individual settlers who were spared because of a personal relationship they had with the Dakota; this was seen in a number of attacks, including Shetek. But whites—settlers, traders, agents, or whatever—were whites, that group of interlopers whom the Dakota believed wanted the land and despised the culture and the people who lived on the land.

Beyond the appearance and language of whites and Indians, there was also a fundamental difference between the two groups. Each saw ownership and property in a different way. The Dakota couldn't comprehend someone who claimed a piece of land as his own and forbade anyone from trespassing on that land. Land, the Dakota believed, was a gift of the Great Spirit to everyone and specifically for no one.

Land for the Dakotas was part of their mystical beliefs. "What makes the earth sacred to the Indian is because the ancestors have returned to the bosom of Mother Earth from which they came. … Fields were plowed and roads and cities built without any regard for the Indians' ancestors."[113]

Then, as nearly every school child knows, is the famous, eloquent, and perhaps apocryphal statement of Chief Seattle about the meaning of land in 1854:

> We will ponder your proposition and when we decide we will let you know. But should we accept it, I here and now make this condition that we will not be denied the privilege without molestation of visiting at any time the tombs of our ancestors, friends, and children. Every part of this soil is sacred in the estimation of my people. Every hillside, every valley, every plain and grove, has been hallowed by some sad or happy event in days long vanished. Even the rocks, which seem to be dumb and dead as they swelter in the sun along the silent shore, thrill with memories of stirring events connected with the lives of my people, and the very dust upon which you now stand responds more lovingly to their footsteps than yours, because it is rich with the blood of our ancestors, and our bare feet are conscious of the sympathetic touch. Our departed braves, fond mothers, glad, happy hearted maidens, and even the little children who lived here and rejoiced here for a brief season, will love these somber solitudes and at eventide they greet shadowy returning spirits. And when the last Red Man shall have perished, and the memory of my tribe shall have become a myth among the White Men, these shores will swarm with the invisible dead of my tribe, and when your children's children think themselves alone in the field, the store, the shop, upon the highway, or in the silence of the pathless woods, they will not be alone. In all the earth there is no place dedicat-

[113]   Lawrence, Elden. 2008. *Stories and Reflections from an Indian Perspective.* Sioux Falls, SD: Pine Hill Press, p. 84

ed to solitude. At night when the streets of your cities and villages are silent and you think them deserted, they will throng with the returning hosts that once filled them and still love this beautiful land. The White Man will never be alone.

But for the settlers and immigrants the ownership of land was the whole point of settling—to own that land, to farm that land, and to pass that land on to the next generation. Nor did the two groups understand each other about the nature of personal possessions. When the Dakota came into the settlers' homes and asked for food or supplies, the settlers despised them as lazy beggars and sometimes they punished the Dakota for stealing. For a Dakota such a refusal to share broke the sense of a community and was foreign to their sense of sharing and giving away their possessions. Thus what faced the settlers at Shetek and in other areas of southern Minnesota was a difference, not just in language or appearance, but a fundamental difference of belief. Even though many whites could speak Dakota and many Dakota spoke English, they still could not understand each other about certain basic issues.

What happened at Shetek may have been a result of such a misunderstanding. The events on that Wednesday began rather innocuously but those events escalated into a terrible butchering of women and children. Whatever the intent, if indeed there was conscious intent by the Dakota Indians, what happened that Wednesday became history and it is often used as a signature event of the 1862 War.

It began in the northern part of the settlement on August 20th.

The Attack at Shetek

Aaron Myers (Meyers), age 36 and his wife Mary, also 36, and their five children came to the lake in 1857 where Aaron built his cabin on the north end of the lake [NW ¼, Section 20, Shetek Twnshp]. He had originally come from New York and settled briefly in Wisconsin. He then "caught the Dakota Fever"[114] and went west into the Minnesota Territory. He had first settled in Lyon County near what would become the village of Saratoga in order to trap and trade with the Dakota. When one of the residents of Saratoga was killed by the Dakota, he left the area and settled on Section 20 of what later became Shetek Township.[115] Workman describes him as a small, robust, well-preserved man with a good memory when Workman interviewed him in the late 1800s. The eldest child, Louisa, age 12, was away at school in Cottonwood that day. The four youngest, Arthur (11), Olive (8), Fred (6), and Addie (1) were at home. Aaron Myers was called the "doctor" by the Dakota because he treated some of them with herbal

---

[114] Myers nd, 2

[115] Luehmann, Maxine Kayser. 1982. *The Sun and the Moon, A History of Murray County. [Minnesota]*: Murray County Board of Commissioners.

recipes; he was also apparently fluent in Dakota. Perhaps this friendly relationship spared the family.[116]

Living with the Myer family was Edgar Bently, a 30-year old single man. He had come to the lake the year before and was employed by William Everett to work in mill that Everett was planning to build.

The sun rose that day at 5:30 a.m. (A timeline of the events the first day at Shetek can be found in Plate 11.) The Dakota appeared at that time or earlier. They broke through a fence bordering Myer's corn field and began riding through the field. Myers ordered them to leave. One account has an Dakota raising his gun to shoot Myers, but another Dakota stopped him by reminding his fellow tribesman of the help that Myers had given them. The Dakota left the field. Myers returned to his cabin and loaded personal possessions and his family on an ox-drawn wagon. At this time his wife was very ill of pneumonia. Before he left, he sent his son Arthur to the Hurd cabin, about ¾ a mile away. The boy came back and told his father that the Hurd cabin was deserted and John Voight, who was staying with the Hurds, was lying dead outside the cabin. Myers, now convinced that his family was in danger, fled north and east to Charles Zierke's (Dutch Charley) cabin. The cabin was empty, Charles Zierke having left earlier in the day for New Ulm apparently because he had been warned by Rhodes who had fled Slaughter Slough when the firing began. Edgar Bently either was at the Everett cabin when the Dakota came or he went south when the Myers went east. He survived Slaughter Slough and caught up with the Myers after they had arrived at Dutch Charley's later that day.

The Dakota Indians stayed only briefly at the Myers' cabin, and after warning the Myers to flee, the Dakota went south traveling less than a mile to the Phineas Hurd cabin [SW ¼. Section 20, Shetek Twnshp]. Phineas had come to the lake in 1859 with his 26-year old wife, Alomina (Hamm). They had two children, both or whom may have been born at the lake, William Henry (3) and an infant.[117]

A William Jones came with the Hurds when they moved from South Bend (near Mankato) to Lake Shetek. It was said that Jones had deserted his wife in Mankato, taking the furniture and farm animals to Shetek. Also living with the Hurds was a John Voigt (Voight) who was a partner with another settler at Shetek, H.G. Koch. Voigt had come to Shetek with Koch in 1862 and was known as a quick-tempered person who had previously quarreled with the Dakota.

Early in June 1862 Phineas Hurd and William Jones left Shetek to go to the Dakota Territory. They might have been on some kind of hunting or trading expedition or some sources indicate that they went to the Dakota Territory to determine the prospects for settling there because of the blackbird infestation in

---

[116] "Myers was known among the Indians as Siha Siarinna (Small Feet). He was also called Doctor because he successfully treated several of the Indians who had sore eyes and also took care of those who were sick or injured. He became well-known among the natives who frequented the vicinity." Arthur Rose, *Illustrated History of Lyon County Minnesota.* Marshall, MN: Northern History Publishing Co., 1912, p. 35

[117] Alomina never names the baby in her April 28, 1862 statement to the claims adjustment commissioners. (Bryant and Murch, 1864, 367 ff.) The 1860 US Census has her name as Christine. The name "Charlie" is also sometimes found.

southern Minnesota. They took with them a wagon and a team of horses. Hurd left John Voigt in charge of the farm. One of the Dakota who raided the cabins at Shetek in August 1862 was riding a horse that some settlers identified as belong to Hurd or Jones. Mrs. Hurd recounted that observation in her testimony to the commissioners, and because neither Phineas Hurd nor Jones was ever heard from again, nor were their bodies found, it is assumed they were either killed by the Dakota or had died in some kind of accident in the Dakota Territory.

On that morning of the 20th when the Dakota Indians came to the Hurd cabin around 6:00 a.m., they found Mrs. Hurd milking, John Voigt out of bed, and two sleeping children. Hibschman,[118] taking his information from an account of Mrs. Hurd, in flowery language and likely embellishing and adding details, described what happened next:

> When Mrs. Hurd had finished her milking she started for the house with her pail. As she approached the ponies of the Indians, a dog ran out from them, and, joyfully barking, rushed upon her with the impetuosity peculiar to his kind when a long-lost friend is found. She immediately recognized her husband's dog and eagerly looked around, expecting Mr. Hurd to be near. But as her eyes roved through the surrounding trees and back again to the house, they fell upon the ponies of the Indians; and her milk pail slipped from her hand, her hair turned to a lighter shade, and her heart almost stood still as she discovered among them the pony upon which her husband had left for the Missouri. At last she had found the horse and dog. But where was her husband? In an instant the imagination of the true wife pictured his death at the stake with the red demons yelling around him, while, amid the smoke, his soul arose to the sky.
>
> Other Indians now appeared from the woods, and, rushing into the house and barn, began to plunder and destroy everything in sight, while the small crowd surrounding Mrs. Hurd, who stood mutely watching with her fatherless, homeless children pressed to her breast, debated the question of her disposal. At length one of them stepped to her side, roughly took hold of her arm, turned her towards the open prairie, and pointing away from the settlement, said, with warning in his voice: "White squaw go to her mother."

The noise of their arrival woke the infant and the child began to cry. John Voigt picked up the baby and carried it outside. At this point one of the Dakota shot and killed him. Then as Mrs. Hurd described above, the Dakota ransacked the cabin, destroying and stealing the contents.[119]

---

[118] Hibschman, H.J. 1901. The Shetek Pioneers and the Indians. Typed manuscript. Shetek Collection, Brown County Museum, Brown County Historical Society, New Ulm, MN, p. 12

[119] She also notes in her account to the commissioners that they had 200 pounds of butter and 23 cheeses which the Indians destroyed and for which she sought reparations. This seems a rather generous supply of butter and cheese, but the compiler of her account included an opinion that she would likely receive the reparations. These monies were paid out of the annuities which ordinarily would have been given to the Dakota, because by this time (June 1863) the treaties had been revoked and the annuities stopped.

The Dakota then told Mrs. Hurd to take her children and leave Shetek. She should go directly across the prairie to New Ulm. The Dakota did not want her to go to the south end of the lake to get to the New Ulm–Sioux Falls post road because they did not want her to warn the other settlers. She quickly gathered some clothing for the children and to ensure that she would not go south along the lake, the Dakota escorted her three miles east from her cabin. Thus, although Voigt was killed and the Dakota told her the other settlers would die, she and her children escaped. In her testimony, Mrs. Hurd attributed her and her children's survival to her acquaintance with the Dakota, her ability to speak their language, and her treating the Dakota with kindness.

But she and a 3-year old and an infant were 60 miles from New Ulm, the nearest town, without shoes for the three-year old and without food for any of them, and she was uncertain of the route. (Plate 12 shows the route that Alomina Hurd and her children followed.) She describes her feelings:

> It was clear, and the sun shone with more than usual brightness. The dew on the grass was heavy. My little boy, William Henry, being barefooted and thinly clad, shivered with the cold, and, pressing close to me, entreated me to return to our home…. I insisted upon going on, enduring the pain and cold of so cheerless a morning. He cried pitifully at first, but, after a time, pressing my hand, he trudged manfully along by my side. The little one rested in my arms, unconscious of our situation.[120]

The next settler to encounter the Dakota may have been Charlie Hatch. Although he lived with the Everetts on the southern end of the lake, in the early morning of the 20th he went north along the lake on an errand. (Plate 13 shows the route of Hatch on that morning.) Hatch was unmarried and 25 at the time. He had come to the lake earlier that year. He was the brother of Almina Hatch Everett, the wife of William Everett. Although Hatch had a claim across Beaver Creek, at the south end of the lake, he apparently was staying with the Everetts.

Before sunrise on the 20th Hatch left the Everett cabin and headed north along the lake to the Hurd cabin, about five miles north. He passed the Dakota camp near the Wrights, but saw nothing amiss. He crossed the "outlet," probably Bloody Lake, a lake connected to Lake Shetek, and arrived at the Hurd cabin. There he found the body of John Voight and a ransacked and deserted cabin. Hatch turned around and retraced his steps. As he came near the Koch cabin, just south of Bloody Lake, he saw Dakota and heard gunfire. Avoiding the cabin and the danger of the Dakota, Hatch continued south along the lake. When he reached the Ireland cabin, he warned the family that the Dakota were attacking the settlers and advised them to flee for their lives. Hatch then continued down the lake stopping at the Ireland, Eastlick, Duley, and Smith cabins warning the settlers of the attack. Charlie Hatch earned the name, the Paul Revere of Lake

---

[120]   Bryant and Murch, 1864, 369-370

Shetek, for a good reason. Each settler, after being warned by Hatch, gathered up his or her family and fled south along the lake.

While Charlie Hatch was returning south after finding Voight dead at the Hurd cabin, the Dakota were also moving around the east side of Bloody Lake, while Hatch was passing along the west side on the narrow peninsula between Lake Shetek and Bloody Lake. The Dakota arrived at the Koch cabin and Hatch heard the gunfire from the cabin.

Andrew Koch[121] and his wife, Mariah (Maria) age 29, together with E.G. Koch, who was no relation, were living in that cabin [SW ¼. Section 29, Shetek Twnshp].

E.G. Koch, 29, was an unmarried trapper and trader at Shetek. He had gone to St. Peter to obtain supplies. While there he had heard of the uprising, probably on Tuesday, August 19. He then went up river to Mankato and then to New Ulm, arriving there on Thursday or Friday. He took part in the battle for New Ulm on Saturday.

Andrew Koch and his wife Maria (they had no children) were the only two facing the Dakota as they arrived. Mariah who was born in Prussia in 1832 came to Shetek with her husband in 1858.[122] Maria was described as a strong, stocky German woman, bright, neat, and clean. She, according to the account, was the kind of person who, when you entered her home, you felt you should leave your shoes outside.[123] One account has Maria in a field keeping birds away from the grain when the Dakota arrived. They rode into the field, took her gun, and ordered her to leave. According to Oehler,[124] Maria, deprived of her gun, went south along the lake and joined up with the other settlers at the Wright cabin. Meanwhile, the Dakota rode up to the cabin and ordered Andrew to get water; as he was going for the water, they shot and killed him. This was probably the gunfire that Charlie Hatch heard. The Dakota then ransacked the cabin.

---

[121] This name is particularly troublesome. In some accounts his name is spelled Cook. Some narratives imply this is a variant spelling while others contend that the Cooks were an entirely different family who were not living at Shetek. Mariah Koch asserted that the Cooks, a Uriah Cook and a Moses Cook, were not at Lake Shetek (Workman, Harper. 1924. Early History of Lake Shetek County. An unpublished typed manuscript. Shetek Collection, Brown County Museum, Brown County Historical Society, New Ulm, MN.). Myers, however, in a letter to Neil Currie (11/20/1894) claimed that Cook and Koch were the same person. There probably were memory lapses or transcription errors in some of the accounts. There is also a Kock spelling in some accounts. For consistency, the name here is spelled Koch.

[122] Information about Mr. Koch is found in the Curie papers in a document entitled "Incidents of the Indian Massacre as Told by Mrs. Koch." In that document she claimed that Inkpaduta of the Spirit Lake massacre was at Lake Shetek in 1859/60. She also describes in some detail the treatment of the captives who were taken at Lake Shetek.

[123] Workman 1924

[124] 1959, 106. There is some difficulty accepting Oehler's account entirely. His book occupies a grey area between history and fiction. He invents many conversations without reference to sources and his speculation often overcomes the evidence. Oehler has Mariah Koch captured by White Lodge after the fighting at Slaughter Slough. White Lodge, however, was the leader of the group of Dakota who took the Shetek captives into the Dakota Territory and we know Mrs. Koch was not among that group.

The cabin just to the south of the Koch cabin was occupied by Thomas Ireland (50), his second wife Sophia, and their four daughters, Rosana (9), Eillen (7), Sarah Jane (5), and Julianne (3) [NE ¼. Section 22, Shetek Twnshp[125]]. Thomas Ireland was a tall man, 6'3", a good talker and hard working. He had come alone to the lake in 1859 and his family joined him in 1860 (1861). He was born in Pennsylvania in 1812. He married Sarah Harrison in 1834. She died in 1843 and he remarried in 1850 to Sophia Walters. He was called "Uncle Tommy" by the other settlers either because of his age or perhaps because of his friendly manner. After the family had been warned by Charlie Hatch, Ireland took his gun and his family and went to the Wright house with the other settlers.

John Eastlick and his family lived across the section from Ireland, and Lavina describes the Eastlick household:

> On this [the warning by Charlie Hatch], my husband caught little Johnny, our youngest, in his arms, took his two rifles, and started, telling myself and the children to hurry as fast as we could. I took some of my clothes, but my husband told me to leave them. I asked him if I could not get my shoes, even, but he said "no, we have no time to spare," so I started, barefooted, to follow Mr. Eastlick. Rhodes called to me, and asked if I was not going to carry anything. So I went back, and he gave me some powder, shot and lead. I took it in the skirt of my dress, and started as fast as I could run; and that was but slowly, for my limbs seemed very heavy, and the pieces of lead kept falling to the ground every few rods. I felt so perfectly unnerved with fear that I gave up, and told John, my husband, that I could not go much further. He urged me to keep on, and support myself by holding to his coat. This I did not do, but told him if he would go slowly, I would try to get to Mr. Smith's with him.[126]

The next household was the Duly/Duley family. William Duley is one of the more complex characters in this saga. Satterlee says,

> There is something peculiar about this man's adventures. Lean Bear was killed by a settler whom he tried to warn of danger, and it is claimed that Duley killed him. He is said to have joined Elijah Whiton on the way to New Ulm; they were attacked and Whiton was killed, but Duley again escaped without harm. He was selected to cut the rope on the drop which hung the Dakota at Mankato, and was so frightened he succeeded only by accident. An officer describes him as the 'blackest white man he ever saw.' [Satterlee] also says he missed the rope at the signal and accidentally touched the taut rope in his excitement, severing it.[127]

---

[125] This location does not correspond to other maps.

[126] Eastlick 1864, p. 7.

[127] Satterlee 1915, 51-52

But all this was later. However the other settlers viewed him, on August 20th he and his family joined them as they fled south to the Wright cabin.

Just south of the small lake adjoining Shetek was the cabin of Henry and Julia Smith [NE ¼, Section 7, Murray Twnshp[128]]. Henry and Julia had come to Shetek in 1855 and saw themselves as one of the first settlers; they had no children. When they were warned by Charlie Hatch, they also made their way south along the lake to the Wright cabin. They must have left quickly because when the Eastlicks came to the Smith cabin they found it deserted. The refugees now numbered 24: Mariah Koch, six members of the Ireland family, seven members of the Eastlick family, Rhodes, seven members of the Duley family and Mr. and Mrs. Smith. The Wright cabin was a half mile south of the Smith cabin.

William and Almira Everett with their three children had settled on the lower end of Lake Shetek [NW ¼. Section 12, Murray Twnshp[129]]. Their cabin was on the south side of Beaver Creek, which runs into the Des Moines River on the south end of Lake Shetek. Everett had plans for building a saw mill and flour mill on the river. Today there is a dam on the Des Moines River about 500 yards south of the location of the Everett cabin. Charlie Hatch, Almira's brother, lived with them and he likely also warned them of what was happening on the northern part of the lake. They made their way north to the Wright cabin, about a half-mile away.

The settlers converged on the Wright cabin. According to Johansson's chronology, it was around 9:00 a.m. when the settlers arrived at the cabin.

John and Julia Wright had come to Shetek in 1859. They had built their home east of the lake [SW ¼. Section 8, Murray Twnshp]. It was likely the largest and most imposing of the settlers' homes. It was a two-storey structure, built of heavy logs, longer and sturdier than the other buildings in the lake area. That was likely the reason the other settlers headed there. The Dakota camp of Pawn was nearby. John Wright had gone to Mankato/Lake Crystal and he had asked Charlie Hatch and Thomas Ireland to look after the farm and his wife Julia and their two children, Dora (6), and George (4).

Julia Wright was described as a good and kind woman. John, her husband, was characterized as "disreputable." The Dakota name for him was "Tonka Tensena," Big Liar. After the fighting at Slaughter Slough, Mrs. Wright was taken captive and after her release, John Wright divorced her because she had been raped by the Dakota and had become pregnant. John Wright felt she should have resisted more forcefully. He lived with her until the child was born and when he saw the child was part Dakota, he left her. This particularly sordid behavior was tracked down by Workman. An unsupported story has her going to Nebraska with the mixed-blood child.

Thirty-four people were now in the cabin: Maria Koch, Thomas Ireland, Sophia Ireland, Rosana Ireland, Ellen Ireland, Sarah Ireland, Julianne Ireland, John Eastlick, Lavina Eastlick, Merton Eastlick, Frederick Eastlick, Franklin Eastlick,

---

128   The small lake now has the name of the family, Smith Lake

129   This location does not correspond to other maps.

Giles Eastlick, Johnnie Eastlick, Mr. Rhodes, William Duley, Laura Duley, William Duley, Jr., Emma Duley, Jefferson (John) Duley, Bell Duley, Francis Duley, Henry Smith, Sophia Smith, Sophia Wright, Dora Wright, George Wright, William Everett, Almina Everett, Ablillian Everett, Willie Everett, Charley Everett, Charley Hatch, and Edgar Bently. The number of persons sometimes varies with a particular account, but 34 is also the number given by Lavina Eastlick.

It must have been a terrified and confused group of eight men, seven women, and nineteen children, eleven of whom were younger than six. Mrs. Koch was undoubtedly distraught having left her husband dead in front of their cabin. Charlie Hatch had seen the dead bodies of his neighbors. Mrs. Koch and Mrs. Wright were without their husbands. Others would be telling their own stories of their escape and the looting and destruction the Dakotas brought to their homes. Mothers and fathers were desperately watching out for their children.

To confuse matters even further, there was also a small band of Dakota who were just outside and inside the cabin. Mrs. Eastlick said there were about a dozen Dakota led by Pawn. These Dakota, according to Mrs. Eastlick, were inside the Wright house and they told the whites that they would fight with them against the hostile Dakota who were coming down along the lake after having looted the cabins.

The hostile Dakota, probably about two dozen, made their appearance around the time the settlers got to the Wright house, midmorning. The whites and the group of Dakota led by Pawn fired several shots which were returned by the Dakota surrounding the cabin. This desultory firing continued for several hours.

The scene inside the cabin must have been rather chaotic: guns firing, children crying, women loading weapons. The white settlers probably were confused and distrustful of Pawn's group inside the cabin while they were firing at the Dakota outside the cabin.[130] The settlers probably kept a wary eye on the Dakota in the cabin while shooting at the occasional Dakota outside the cabin.[131] The Dakota outside the cabin returned the fire but they did not rush the cabin. The women inside reloaded the men's weapons or fired their own guns. (We know Mrs. Koch had picked up her husband's gun and brought it to the cabin.) The nineteen children would have been hiding, wherever they could to avoid the bullets, perhaps on the second floor. They would have been terrified and the younger ones would likely have been crying. The men would also have been worried; they weren't soldiers and their only experience of firing a gun was when they shot game for their families. The guns were muzzle loaders, which required time, particularly by untrained persons, to load. Those muzzle loaders which were not rifled would have been inaccurate at any distance and even the rifled guns, in untrained hands,

---

[130] Mrs. Eastlick said she distrusted Pawn's group. She advised her husband not to fire his gun until after Pawn's group had fired, lest these Dakota turn on the whites when their guns were empty. Obviously, when she writes about her suspicions (Eastlick, 1864, p. 9), she is writing after Pawn's Dakota had betrayed the whites. Her premonitions may or may not have been as strong as she describes.

[131] Oehler has one of his constructed dialogues on this: "Pawn urged the whites to shoot off their guns. 'That will scare the bad Indians. They will be afraid to come near.' 'Do you think we are fools?' snapped a settler. 'We will keep our guns loaded and cocked.'" (Oehler 1959, p. 107)

would likely miss a person over 50 yards away. Many of the guns were shotguns with even less range and accuracy. The Wright cabin was substantial, but it was of wood and if the Dakota set it on fire, all in the cabin would have to flee into the gunfire of the waiting Dakota. Pawn, when he returned from one of his parleys with the Dakota who surrounded the cabin, told the settlers that there were 200 hostile Dakota surrounding the house.

Pawn also told the settlers that the Dakota surrounding the cabin said they would not harm the settlers if they would leave. But if not, they would set fire to the cabin. After a brief discussion, the settlers decided to leave the cabin.

The decision to leave the cabin must have been difficult. Because the decision to leave the cabin led to Slaughter Slough, it may appear in hindsight that the settlers should have remained in the cabin and fought it out. But that also might have been a bad decision. The settlers had no hope of rescue; no one outside of Shetek knew what was happening there; they were in a situation similar to the settlers at the Spirit Lake killings in 1857. Any supplies in the cabin would not have lasted long with 34 persons. One torch would have driven them out. There were no good choices and the decision to leave seemed to the settlers to be the best one.[132]

The decision made, the 34 refugees left the Wright cabin. The mail route from Sioux Falls to New Ulm went just south of Lake Shetek. Like most trails or routes in the mid-1900s, it was a trail that was visible, but it was hardly a road. It likely had wheel ruts which marked the trail. The Wright cabin was probably less than a mile from the route, which was well known to the settlers. They undoubtedly headed for the trail when they left the cabin. Hatch and Rhodes were sent to the Everett cabin to get a wagon, some horses, food, and quilts. The Everett cabin was a half mile south and likely had not yet been looted by the Dakota. The two men returned with the wagon, horses, and supplies. They overtook the other settlers who were on foot and loaded the women and children into the wagon. Mrs. Eastlick, Mrs. Wright, Merton and Frank Eastlick and the eight men ran alongside the wagon.

The flight in the wagon is one of the enduring pictures of the Shetek attack. (See Plate 14.) It was one of the focal pictures in the Stevens Panorama and it appears in many books which describe the event. There is something forebodingly

---

[132] There were other times, such as Sacred Heart and Milford, when the settlers seemed to have a naïve attitude toward the intent of the Dakota. They went back to their homes when told to, they dropped their weapons when asked—and then they were killed. But lest we dismiss the settlers and their ignorance, we should realize that this, too, is a case of, "You had to be there." Previously, the settlers had generally good experiences with the Dakota Indians; they felt (and sadly were wrong) they knew the Dakota. They had never been in battle, they did not know what to do when people held a gun on them, any choice which was not confrontational was the choice to make, and that non-confrontational choice was the choice the settlers generally made. The settlers were not the only ones who misunderstood the Dakota. Sibley sent off a small group of soldiers to bury the dead at the Lower Agency. They and Sibley took little effort to check for hostiles and the result was the near disaster at Birch Coulee. The whites seemed to believe the Dakota were not serious and they underestimated the determination and strength of the Dakota to drive the whites out of Minnesota.

dramatic about the 34 settlers, half of whom are children, running and riding in a wagon to a place called Slaughter Slough.[133]

The Sioux Falls/New Ulm trail may have passed just north or south of the slough. When some of the survivors returned with Workman and Currie to Shetek in 1894, the survivors located the place where the wagon stopped, on the north side of the slough, which they located as NE ¼, Section 3, Township 107, Range 40. The difficulty of locating the trail is that Eastlick's account suggests the wagon left the trail and went north when the Dakota Indians caught up to the fleeing settlers. This fits the Workman description of where the wagon stopped. Johansson, however, in his analysis of the events at Slaughter Slough has the wagon on the south end of the slough. Whether they were on the north or south side, things began to go terribly wrong. There are recollections by three eye-witnesses of that ride and how it ended. Charlie Hatch describes it this way:

> We accordingly hitched up one team, put the women and children into the wagon and started for New Ulm some 75 miles away. We had gone but a few miles, perhaps three or four, when we saw the Indians coming after us, our friendly Indians with the others. They commenced firing on us with fearful effect, the women and children were getting wounded in the wagon so fast that we abandoned it at once and started for the slough and tall grass, firing as we went."[134]

Lavina Eastlick describes it this way:

> So we all started, across the prairie … We traveled over a mile in this manner, when the appalling cry was raised, that the Indians were upon our track. The Indians, who had pretended to be friendly at the house, had deserted us and joined their fellow savages in their demoniac quest of blood and plunder. All was terror and consternation among us; our merciless foes were in sight, riding at their utmost speed, and would soon be upon us. All now got into the wagon that could. Mrs. Smith held the reins, while I, sitting on the fore end of the wagon box, lashed the horses with all my strength, but, with such a load, the poor brutes could not get along faster than a walk. The Indians were fast gaining on us, and the men, thinking it was only the horses they wanted, bade us leave the wagon. We accordingly all jumped out, and ran along as fast as possible, while the men fell in behind to give the women and children what protection they could.[135]

Duley's description emphasizes in a somewhat self-serving manner how he saw his part in the flight:

---

[133] Because the countryside west of Lake Shetek contains many depressions or "sloughs," the location of Slaughter Slough varies on maps. Even the "officially" designated place marked by a plaque indicates that the slough shown by the marker is an approximation of where the slough was. See Plates 10 and 13.

[134] Hatch 1895, 2

[135] Eastlick 1864, p. 10

Old Pond [presumably a misspelling for Pawn] proposed, when we see them plundering Smith's house to go as a friend and see what could be done, all agreed to it. He went out on the prairie and met old Lean Bear and counceled [sic] with him, returned and reported about 40 warriors and that they would burn the house, children and all if we did not leave. This was a trying point, all took fright but Wright [John Wright was not present at Shetek so Duley must be referring to Mrs. Wright] and myself we wanted to hold the house but of course we had to yield to the majority to which I always thought was bad policy, for we had plenty of ammunition and guns and provisions, we could stand a siege. But we abandoned the house and Hatch went and hitched up his two horses to his wagon and intercepted us on the prairie about ¾ of a mile east from Wright's house. We loaded the children in and started to save ourselves, and families from the brutal savages. But oh, they followed us and made the attack, about 30 of them, out on the flat about a mile east of Wright's house. And as they advanced on us we abandoned the wagon, thinking they would desist, but no, they still raised the war whoop; and opened fire, the team took a circular run, bearing to the west, back toward the lake. … At the time Rhodes fired at the crowd and immediately he and Smith broke and fled and the next place I saw them was at Mankato. …. I well remember of urging the women and children on to the slough. My object was to get them in the high grass and stand a[nd] fight.[136]

Pawn and the "friendly" Dakota had now joined the hostile Dakota. The written record, from the perspective of the settlers, tells of the Dakota firing at the wagon. Boutin, in his analysis of the flight, suggests an alternative scenario. In this version, the Dakota, including Pawn and his group, followed the settlers for two miles. They closed in on the settlers, intending to take the horses, but not harm the settlers, as Duley, Hatch, and Eastlick describe. One of the settlers shot Lean/Grizzly Bear, a leader of the Dakota.[137]

The killing of Lean Bear unleashed the killing. The Dakota Indians began firing at the men, women, and children as they abandoned the wagon and ran for the only cover they could see—the tall reeds and grasses along the trail. Who fired first? No one can tell. Boutin[138] claims that if the settlers had not fired, no

---

[136]   This quote was published in the *Murray County Pioneer,* April 12, 1888. It was taken from the manuscript of an unpublished History of Murray County. The title was "Reminiscence of Capt. W.J. Duley." The typewritten account can be found in the Murray County Historical Society Archives in Slayton, Minnesota.

[137]   Who shot Lean/Grizzly Bear, the only documented Dakota casualty? Dahlin (2007, 96) says John Eastlick did, see also a letter from A. Myers to Neil Currie, dated 11/20/1894. Lavina Eastlick says four men fired (1864, p. 11). Oehler (1959, 108) says Duley killed Lean (Grizzy) Bear. Duley says he shot Lean Bear at 75 yards and hit him "one inch below the left nipple" (Duley n.d.). Folwell (1961, 123n Folwell, William Watts. 1961. *A History of Minnesota.* Vol. II. St. Paul, MN: Minnesota Historical Society.) records that Ireland fired the fatal shot. Mrs. Koch (Workman n.d.,43,) says, "I was in the Slough and Eastlick was between his wife and myself when he shot Lean Bear. I know that shot killed him, it was the shooting that located him [Eastlick] and the Indians got him."

[138]   Boutin, Loren Dean. 2006. *Cut Nose Who Stands on a Cloud.* St. Cloud, MN: North Star Press.

one would have been harmed. Others contend that the settlers did fear for their lives, the horses were their property and the only means with which they could reach safety. Thus, shooting to protect the horses was a reasoned choice. Others contend the Dakota wanted more than the horses; they intended all along to kill the settlers. From this vantage point 150 years later, there is no way to tell what might have happened or why things happened as they did. It probably would not have mattered who fired first; the result in any case found its way into the name of the place.

Slaughter Slough

As the settlers ran into the slough several were wounded. Mrs. Eastlick and the children, Julianne Ireland, Emma Duley, and Willie Duley were shot several times. Instead of stopping at the slough, Henry Smith and Rhodes continued running and made their escape, despite the pleas of Smith's wife not to leave. Smith did not stop until he reached Walnut Grove, eleven miles away. There he warned the two brothers of the Dakota attack. He continued on to New Ulm and survived the battle there. Rhodes, who had one of the better rifles given him by John Eastlick, also ran, ignoring calls to leave the rifle. He made his way back to Dutch Charley's, warned him of the Dakota attack, and continued on to Mankato.

Mrs. Eastlick in her account does not name these men nor does she suggest that the men who fled were cowards. She notes approvingly that they warned other settlers of the attack. Satterlee is not so charitable; he says they deserted, "though both well armed."[139] Workman claimed that Everett, Hatch, and Mrs. Kock said, "Duley was a coward, that he was running when they entered the Slough, and never stopped."[140]

Johansson[141] puts the time when the settlers went into the slough at 1:00 p.m. Mrs. Eastlick remembered it as 2:00 p.m.

The Dakota Indians, shooting from higher ground and surrounding the settlers, fired when they heard voices or saw movement. The tall grass, which could have been up to six feet high, made it difficult for the men in the slough to return fire because they would have had to stand and expose themselves to the guns of the Dakota. For two hours the one-sided firing continued. John Eastlick was hit at least twice and the final shot in the head or chest killed him. Mrs. Everett was hit, Lavina Eastlick was hit again, Charles Hatch was shot several times, Sarah Ireland was wounded severely, and Mrs. Smith was hit.

Around 4:00 p.m. Pawn called to the settlers and assured them that the women and children would be safe if they surrendered. Three of the four remaining men were wounded and the women probably saw themselves with no option other than surrender. Almina Everett and Julia Wright stood up and pleaded for

---

[139]   Satterlee 1924 (2001), 51; Satterlee misspells Rhodes name and calls him "Forbes."

[140]   Workman, 1924, 42.

[141]   *Murray County Record*, April 19 1987

their lives and the lives of their children. Tommy Ireland apparently also stood up and was hit with a shotgun blast.

Mrs. Everett and Mrs. Wright were joined by the other women and children and they made their way toward the Dakota. At this point, events become confusing and were interpreted in different ways by different witnesses. One interpretation is that when the women and children surrendered, the Dakota did not harm them. Some they took with them; those became the Shetek captives, while others ran away or succumbed to their wounds and died.[142]

The other interpretation is from the white survivors. In this version, when the women and children came out of the slough, a terrible massacre began and the

Fig. 5: Slaughter Slough Today

description of that killing ground strains the reader's credulity. The men remained in the slough. Eastlick was dead, Ireland and Hatch were badly wounded, and Duley and Bently remained hiding in the grass. Although Duley had a gun and was unwounded (or slightly wounded), he did nothing as his wife and children walked out of the slough. (Duley was the only adult to come out of the fighting without serious wounds.) He still did nothing when the killings began as the children and women came out of the slough.

Lavina Eastlick came out of the slough with four of her sons, Merton carrying Johnny, and Frank and Giles. Freddy stayed hidden in the grass. Julia Wright gathered up the guns and brought them out to the Dakota. Sophia Ireland said goodbye to her wounded husband and joined the others. Sophia Smith, badly wounded in the hip, had difficulty coming out of the slough. Almina Everett, wounded and bleeding, came out. Sarah Ireland, the five-year old who had been shot in the stomach several hours ago, remained in the slough, dying of her wound.

The Dakota began dividing up the captives, one took Mrs. Koch, one took an Ireland child, and another took Lavina Eastlick and Mrs. Duley. Lavina called to Freddy, her five-year old, to join the others. But when he came out of the grass, a Dakota woman clubbed and stabbed him. Frank, her ten-year old, was then shot in the mouth, leg, and stomach. Pawn took Mrs. Wright and her three children and ordered them to get on Charlie Hatch's horse. Almina Everett was shot as she tried to run back to her husband in the slough. William, the Duley's 10-year old son, was shot in front of his mother. Sophia Smith was likely shot again at

---

[142] An example of this interpretation is an interview with the great-grandson of Charles Hatch. In that interview he suggests that the Dakota Indians did not take the Shetek settlers captive; rather the Indians were helping the women and children to survive. (*Return to Shetek*, 2007).

55

this time and died. Merton, seeing what was happening to the others, apparently took Johnnie and ran back into the slough.

A Dakota woman took the end gate of the wagon and beat Belle Duley, the five-year old, to death. The manner and viciousness with which the children were killed varies in some accounts. The *Mankato SemiWeekly Record*, Oct 18, 1862, has this account of Belle Duley's death:

> A little girl of Mrs. Duley's, aged about six years, was brutally murdered by a squaw. The squaw threw the child very hard on the ground, then cut her over the face with a raw-hide whip; then threw her again upon the ground. This hard and brutal treatment did not kill the child, but the savage devil stepped back a few paces and amused herself by throwing a large butcher knife at the child, striking her with it three times, and each time the knife entered her body, inflicted severe wounds, causing immediate death.

There is no source given in the newspaper article for this apparent eye-witness account. Granted that the child was killed, the details of her death, as well as other descriptions in the accounts and in the Stevens's panorama, seem to be inventions or elaborations by someone who wished to embellish the events for its shock value. The reader remains puzzled why the horror of a child being killed needs elaboration.

Mrs. Duley with three of her children, Jefferson (John), Emma, and Francis, were led away. As the Wrights and Duleys were led away, Lavina Eastlick was shot several times (again), perhaps because she was too slow or she hesitated.

Fig. 6: The Base of the Shetek Monument

Then a Dakota came by and beat her severely on her head and shoulder with the butt of his rifle, finally leaving her for dead on the edge of the slough.

But Lavina regained consciousness several hours later. A storm has passed through and her clothes were soaked. The Dakota were gone. She heard Merton, her son, calling so she knew he was alive. As she crawled looking for her children, she came upon William Duley who was dying, she found Willie Everett and his sister Lillian, the bodies of Mrs. Sophia Smith and Mrs. Sophia Ireland, both dead. Julianne Ireland, two years old, was lying sleeping on her mother's breast. Lavina also found her two-year old son, Giles, dead and a few feet further her other son, Freddie, dying of the beating he received. She also came upon Almina Everett, dying of a shot to the lungs.

There is something almost surreal in Lavina Eastlick's description of her painful journey through that morgue of the dead and dying. As the sun set, Lavina crawled through the wet grass coming upon women and children, some of whom were her own, dead or dying. She herself was severely wounded and unable to help. Although Mrs. Smith and Mrs. Ireland were dead, she did arrange their bodies, and took an apron from one of the women to shield her own body from the rain. She reflected on the sufferings of those poor souls she found, but she took comfort in her faith in a better life in heaven for those who died. She kept going because she believed her other two sons, Merton and Johnnie, were still alive and near. She continued this aimless wandering search for the rest of the night.

Thus ends the first day of the death and suffering at Shetek. At the close of Wednesday, August 20, 1862, there were three groups at Shetek, the dead/dying, the captives, and the refugees. Twelve are dead or dying in the slough: Belle Duley (5) and William Duley Jr. (10); Freddy Eastlick (4), Giles Eastlick (8), and John Eastlick, their father; Willie Everett (5), Charley Everett (2), and Almina Everett, their mother; Julianne Ireland (3), Sarah Ireland (5), and Sophie Ireland, their mother; and Sophia Smith. In the slough, alive but wounded, are five adults and two children: Edgar Bently (slightly wounded), William Duley (perhaps not wounded), William Everett (badly wounded), Lavina Eastlick (badly wounded), Merton Eastlick (not wounded), Johnnie Eastlick (not wounded), and Charley Hatch (badly wounded). Mr. Rhodes and Henry Smith escaped before the massacre and were unhurt. There were three adults and nine children taken captive: Mrs. Maria/Christina Koch, Mrs. Laura Duley, Mrs. Julia Wright, Rosana Ireland, Ellen Ireland, Jefferson (John) Duley, Francis Duley, Emma Duley, Frank Eastlick,[143] Dora Wright, and George Wright. The following morning the Dakota returned to loot the dead and they found three children still alive. They took Lillian Everett captive and the other two, Charles Everett and one of the Ireland children., they left to die in the slough. There was also another Wright child, with no first name, listed as an infant, who was captured and later killed. This group was what was later called the "Shetek Captives." (See Plate 13 for a summary of the events.)

Fig. 7: Shetek Monument

---

[143] There is some uncertainty regarding Frank Eastlick, see footnote #164.

V

THE REFUGEES

The cabin of Dutch Charley Zierke, 14 miles east, was the rendezvous for most of the refugees as they made their way east. Zierke's cabin was just north of the New Ulm/Sioux Falls post road. Charley Zierke, born in Germany in 1828, had settled in the northeastern part of Cottonwood County [SE ¼, Section 25, Ann Twnshp) in 1858; he is considered the first settler in the county. In 1960 there apparently was still a depression in the ground marking the location of his cabin. The cabin location was just east of the creek named after him, Dutch Charley's Creek, and a quarter mile northeast of the current Old Westbrook Lutheran Church. The creek revaine is quite deep, probably 40 to 50 feet. A weather-beaten signs marks the spot today.

Dutch Charley was born Karl Zierke. The Dakota gave him the name "Dutch" because they applied that name to anyone who spoke poor English and they called him "Charley" because "k" was not part of the Dakota language.

Zierke's family consisted of his common law wife, Christina (Schumacher), 34, and her three children by a previous marriage, John (11), Henry (8), and Eliza/Louisa, (4). Two daughters had been born to the Zierkes, Mary in 1858 and Anne in 1860. According to the 1860 census the family had 20 acres of unimproved land, four oxen, four milk cows, seven cattle, and four hogs. They took some of their produce to New Ulm to sell, 47 miles to the east. A second couple had homesteaded just south of the Zierkes, but there is no information whether they were still there at the time of the Conflict.

Charley Zierke and his neighbors may have made up a small settlement called New Brunswick, apparently located about six miles north of the present town of Jeffers. Records indicate that there were about a dozen families in this community. The residents apparently either were not there at the time of the War or they fled east as did most of the other settlers in southern Minnesota. Nothing of the village of New Brunswick exists today.

When the 19 settlers fled Shetek, 10 came from Slaughter Slough, three were from the Hurd cabin, and six were from the Myers cabin. All of them made their way eastward to New Ulm or Mankato generally along the post road. There is some uncertainty just where that trail went although there are specific places listed in the accounts that were near that trail. For example, Buffalo Lake, Dutch Charley's cabin, the Brown cabin, and Leavenworth were described as being on or near the post road. There are also places in Cottonwood County where the locals claim the ruts of that road can still be seen. If the post road is traced using these known points, it was about 80 miles from Shetek to New Ulm. The post road was likely longer because it would have gone around sloughs and lakes and it would have crossed the numerous creeks at locations where the banks were less steep and the creek was fordable.

A second issue is that the 19 refugees traveled in six or seven groups or individuals; as these groups or individuals made their way east, they combined or broke apart. Some of the groups were in wagons (Myers) or carriages (Lavina Eastlick), sometimes there was just one young man who traveled quickly (Duley), some were women carrying children (Hurd), some were children traveling alone (Johnnie and Merton Eastlick). The time that it took the refugees to reach New Ulm or Mankato varied widely. One group made it in two days while another group took two weeks.

Another difficulty in tracing the routes is that the first-hand accounts don't always say when a particular group or individual was at a specific place on the post road. Many of the accounts were written long after the events and the blurring of places and dates that occur over time in a person's memory likely affected the accuracy of those accounts.

Finally, there is evidence of selective memory on the part of some authors and at times the reader even questions the veracity of a particular author. Mrs. Hurd first told her story, and it was written down at that time, to the reparations committee which had the task of determining the amount of money that was to be paid to those who lost property during the conflict. Although Mrs. Hurd likely did not slant her story for the reparations committee, she did have an emotional impact on the commissioners and she did detail her loses quite carefully. Lavina Eastlick was a survivor, before, during, and after the events of Shetek. She made a comfortable income promoting and selling her account of the events of Shetek. She wrote her story in a dramatic, emotional, and personal style that appealed to readers of that time (although it is sometimes tedious to the modern reader). Some never shared their experiences. John Wright refused to provide information on Shetek or on his family, probably reflecting his behavior when his wife returned from captivity. Then there is William Duley. In his account, he was the one who shot Lean Bear, he left the slough at the encouragement of the wounded in order to get help, he survived by his own wits and skill when those with him on the escape to New Ulm died. He played an important part in the defense of New Ulm. He cut the rope at the hanging of the 38 Dakota in Mankato. He spent a good share of his life after Shetek badgering the federal government to pay him compensation and a pension even though he had not served in the regular army. Satterlee may have been accurate in his characterization of Duley.

Thus with a dozen caveats, this is the story of the refugees.[144]

Rhodes, Smith, Zierke

Rhodes, together with Henry Smith, left the slough when the wagon stopped and the settlers ran into the slough. Abandoning his wife, Smith went on to Plum Creek, near present-day Walnut Grove and warned two young men, Daniel and John Burns, of the Dakota attack.

---

[144] The many groups and the varying speed makes the story a bit difficult to follow. There is a timeline in Appendix C that may help (or exacerbate the confusion).

Fig. 8: Dutch Charlie Location, Ann Twnshp, Cotton-wood County

In Johansson's chronology Smith would have left around 1:00 p.m. He traveled the 10 miles to Plum Creek in two hours and went with the Burns brothers to Lamberton, another ten miles. They reached Lamberton on the evening of the same day, Wednesday, August 20. On Thursday the three men continued to the Brown cabin, another 20 miles. Smith then apparently left the brothers because the next day the Burns met up with Dutch Charley's family and Rhodes somewhere around Leavenworth. Smith is not mentioned in this reunion.

When Rhodes left the slough, he went northeast to Dutch Charley's cabin. It would have taken him some four hours to make the 15 miles so he would have gotten there in the late afternoon. When Rhodes told him of the attack, Zierke gathered his wife and five children together with some possessions, loaded them into a wagon, and with Rhodes followed the post road northeast to New Ulm. They traveled all night in a drizzling rain and on Thursday they reached the Brown cabin, 25 miles down the road. The cabin was deserted and the windows were broken. Five miles further along the trail they found the dead and mutilated bodies of Jonathan Brown, his father Joseph, and his sister Horatia.

The next day, Friday, Zierke and Rhodes got within eight miles of New Ulm. Zierke left his family and Rhodes to look for food (or to scout ahead or he deserted them, depending on the particular account). While Zierke was absent, a small group of Dakota found the Zierke family and Rhodes. Mrs. Zierke talked them out of killing them and she, Rhodes, and the five children were taken captive. The Dakota led them away, but ten miles further the Dakota saw a scouting party sent out from New Ulm by Charles Flandrau, the commander the troops defending New Ulm. The Dakota told the captives to hide in the woods, while they also went and hid. The captives hid, but when the Dakota did not return, Rhodes, Mrs. Zierke, and the children retraced their steps to a cabin they had passed. (Yes, there is something very strange in this story—the captors telling their captives to hide, which they did so those who could rescue them could not see them.) There is no description of where this cabin was; it may have been near Leavenworth. They remained in this cabin through Saturday (23rd), Sunday (24th), and Monday (25th), avoiding any Dakota they saw. They tried again to reach New Ulm, but the destruction and dead bodies in the countryside frightened them and they returned to their hiding place. They stayed there until the following Saturday when they continued their journey to Mankato. They arrived on Sunday (31st). Charley Zierke had gotten into New Ulm when he left his family, but the second battle of New Ulm on Saturday (23rd) had prevented him from returning. He was evacuated with the rest of New Ulm on Monday and went to

Mankato. There he was reunited with his family when they came six days later. Rhodes left Mankato shortly after and enlisted in the army.

The Zierke family moved to New Ulm later in 1862 and in 1863 a son was born, but their two daughters, Anne and Mary, died. In 1865 Charley Zierke died of jaundice and was buried in the New Ulm cemetery, although there is no record of his burial or tombstone marking his grave.

Everett, Bently, Hatch, Myers

After this, the story of the refugees gets more complicated. When the fighting at the slough ended, around 3:00 p.m. (Wednesday afternoon), William Everett, Edgar Bently, and Charlie Hatch left the slough. Everett has been shot three times, Hatch three times, and Bently once. By this time, the women and children had either surrendered or been killed, and the men apparently decided that their only option was to go east. They traveled the fifteen miles to Dutch Charley's, reaching there at night. With their wounds, on foot, it probably took them eight or nine hours.

When they arrived at the cabin, Dutch Charley and his family had already left with Rhodes, but Aaron Myers, his wife Mary, and their four children were in the cabin. The Myers, whose cabin was on the north end of the lake, had been spared by the Dakota who told them to leave the lake and go east. They left with a wagon filled with their children and some provisions Wednesday morning. They reached Dutch Charley's by going directly east (some 17 miles) and reached the cabin around 10:00 p.m. Their progress was slow, perhaps because they went across the prairie rather than by road.

The next morning (Thursday) the five adults and four children traveled to the Brown cabin (30 miles). The cabin was vacant and they found the bodies of the Brown family between the cabin and Leavenworth. They arrived at Leavenworth at dusk. The total journey that day was around 45 miles in 12 to 14 hours, assuming they left Zierke's at daybreak. The wounded men would likely have ridden in the wagon and they apparently made good time.

The residents of Leavenworth had deserted the village and the refugees could hear cannons firing from the direction of Fort Ridgely, 17 miles to the north. If the refugees had indeed reached Leavenworth on Thursday, they would not likely have heard cannon fire. Ridgely was attacked on Wednesday and Friday, but not on Thursday. The Myer party could have heard gunfire, perhaps practice rounds, or the date of their arrival at Leavenworth may be wrong. If they reached Leavenworth on Friday, they would likely have heard sounds of the battle from Fort Ridgely.

Also on that Thursday, a rescue party had been sent out from New Ulm. George Tousely was in command of the group and they went out to rescue a group of eleven persons hiding in a ravine near Leavenworth. The rescue party came within four miles of Leavenworth, turned around, and returned to New Ulm, arriving there around 1:00 Friday. If the Myers party did reach Leavenworth on Thursday, they would have come very close to being rescued.

Friday, or more likely Saturday, the Myers party continued to New Ulm; they stopped just south of New Ulm on a bluff. They heard gunfire and saw the smoke of the burning town (which would suggest that that date was Saturday when New Ulm was being attacked.) Aaron Myers left his family and ran into New Ulm, breaking through the Dakota lines surrounding the town. When he got into New Ulm, he found John Wright and they joined in the defense of New Ulm.

Meanwhile, Everett, Bently, Hatch, Mrs. Myers and the children camped that evening and the next day (Sunday) waiting for Aaron Myers to return. On Monday they decided to continue to Mankato. They camped that evening near a lake where they found food. On Tuesday, they got a fresh set of oxen and continued to Mankato. In late afternoon they came upon some mounted men from Capt. Dane's cavalry. On Friday they arrived in Mankato. (The dates are a bit unclear, because the Friday arrival has to fit with the death of Mrs. Myers, but it seems strange that after meeting Dane, they did not make better time to Mankato.) Mrs. Myers had been ailing the entire trip and she died that night.

Aaron Myers left New Ulm on Sunday, crossed the Minnesota River with Mr. Tuttle[145] and John Wright and went to St. Peter. On Tuesday, Myers was united with his eldest daughter, Louisa, who was away at school when the Dakota attacked Shetek. In St. Peter Myers also met Duley, Smith, and Rhodes. On Friday, he went to Mankato where he was reunited with his wife and the other children. He was at the side of his wife when she died.

Eastlick, Hurd

The last group included Lavina Eastlick, Merton and Johnnie Eastlick, Tommy Ireland, and Mrs. Hurd and her two children. When the women and children surrendered at Slaughter Slough and together with their children they went to the Dakota Indians, Lavina Eastlick and her children also came out. Lavina was shot several times and beaten and left for dead. She had told Merton that he was to care for his younger brother Johnnie. Frederick, Giles, and her husband John were dead or dying, Frank, her other son, was badly wounded.

Merton and Johnnie ran back to the slough when the killing of the women and children began. They remained there until late afternoon. They came upon Thomas Ireland who had been shot in the lungs and seemed near his end. But he crawled along with Merton and Johnnie for a half mile and then he told them to go on because he could no longer keep up with them. Merton took Johnny and left him, but not, as Hibschman notes, before kissing him good-bye. That evening

---

[145] This "Mr. Tuttle" is only mentioned by Aaron Myers in his "Reminiscence and Biographical Data" (1900, 1906, Dakota Conflict of 1862 Manuscript Collections, microfilm, Minnesota Historical Society). He does not provide a first name. There was a William Tuttle living in the Leavenworth area, but he was killed on August 19th as part of the Leavenworth Rescue Expedition. There were other Tuttles in Mankato, but there is no Tuttle listed on any of the volunteer groups that came to New Ulm. Myers may have been wrong about the name.

the boys slept on the prairie where their sleep was disturbed by wolves. Hibschman[146], again with those flowery words, describes that night:

> What a night of terror it must have been for the eleven-year-old boy! After darkness the hideous noise of the wolves came to his ears. At first they seemed far away; but after a while the shivering little sentinel could see their fiery eyes glittering behind the trees close by. He shouted and they scampered away. But they soon came back again; and his little heart almost broke as the horrible thought took shape in his mind that they would like to eat him and his baby brother. Again he shouted, and again the cowards left But at intervals through the night they returned and wickedly blinked at the watchful Merton, who at the first peep of dawn awakened his charge and went out into the trail.[147]
> (See Plate 16.)

On Thursday, the boys continued on the trail to Buffalo Lake and stayed there over night. The next morning they continued on to Dutch Charley's. Around five in the afternoon they caught up with Alomina Hurd and her two children. The five of them slept in a corn field near Dutch Charley's.

After being shot and beaten[148] Lavina Eastlick crawled around the slough finding dead and dying men, women, and children. The next morning (Thursday) she continued her painful journey. (See Plate 17.) She heard the cries of children in the morning and afternoon, as well as gunshots. In the evening she moved toward some timber and kept crawling, believing she would soon come upon Dutch Charley's cabin. Friday morning, however, she realized she had traveled in a circle because she was back at Lake Shetek. She went to Tommy Ireland's deserted cabin and found some food. When night fell she went southeast in search of the

---

[146] Hibschman, H.J. 1901. The Shetek Pioneers and the Indians. Typed manuscript. Shetek Collection, Brown County Museum, Brown County Historical Society, New Ulm, MN, p. 28.

[147] Some readers may ponder on the accuracy of Merton and Johnnie's adventures in their journey from Shetek to the Brown's cabin. Did Merton embellish his story? Did Lavina add details, although she does not include the wolf account? Did other writers such as Hibschmann make up the story? But there is always a core in such stories. Merton must have told his mother and John Stevens about the wolves. Newspaper reporters who interviewed Merton must have heard something on which to base their stories. The drama was likely enhanced, in both Hibschmann's words and Stevens's painting. It seems both plausible and in keeping with the other events of Shetek that Merton told what happened to him and Johnnie. It was horrific enough, without adding events.

[148] Lavina, by her account, had been hit four times by bullets. As she fled into the Slough, she was hit with a musket ball in her heel, which caused her much pain. In the Slough she was hit by a musket ball in the side. Then she was struck in the head by a musket ball which lodged between her skull and her scalp. When she came out of the Slough she was shot at from behind, with the musket ball entering the small of her back, exiting just above the hip, and then striking her arm between the elbow and the wrist. None of the wounds seemed fatal, the more serious one through her back must have missed any vital organs. She was then beaten badly with a musket butt on the skull and the shoulders. When she was hospitalized in Mankato, there is no information on how she was treated. Any of the musket balls which remained in her, such as the scalp wound, probably were fairly easily removed. The blows to her head apparently crushed her skull because Laura described how her mother had a place on her head where the skull was missing. She apparently continued to have pain all her life in her heel and arm.

post road. The next day (Saturday) she reached Buffalo Lake and the post road. Around 11:00 a.m. the mail carrier appeared in a carriage; he was traveling to New Ulm and did not realize the Dakota were attacking the settlers. He took her into the carriage and they continued on to Dutch Charley's, arriving there about 4:00 p.m. The house was deserted, except for Tommy Ireland; he had revived after Merton and Johnnie left him and crawled to Dutch Charley's. Ireland told her that Merton and Johnnie were alive and likely ahead of them on the prairie. He joined the mail carrier and Lavina in the carriage and they went eight miles beyond the cabin and camped for the night. On Sunday, the next day, three miles west of the Brown cabin, they saw Mrs. Hurd and her two children struggling along through the prairie. They, too, joined Lavina, Tommy, and the mail carrier in the carriage. A mile further, she saw two figures in the prairie ahead. This is Lavina's account of her reunion with her children:

> She [Mrs. Hurd] was unable to speak for some time, but shook hands with us all, and finally told me that my Merton was a short distance ahead, just out of sight, and was carrying Johnny. I could stay to hear no more, and urging the horse along I soon came up with them. Merton stopped, gazed upon me, but spoke not a word. The mail-carrier took Johnny, who was sleeping, in his arms, and gave him to me; I clasped him to my breast, and, with tears of joy, I thanked God—Oh!, how fervently—for sparing my children thus far. How I longed to press to my bosom my poor Merton, but could not, for I was unable to get off the sulky; all I could do was to press his wasted hand, and call him my dear brave boy. He, though only eleven years old, had carried the child, who was fifteen months old, fifty miles, but now he could hardly stand alone; for he felt no fear now, and had nothing to excite him or keep up his strength. He was the poorest person I ever saw, able to stand alone. Two weeks of hard sickness could not have altered his looks more. And little Johnny, too, was sadly changed; his face was entirely covered with a scab, where the mosquitos [sic] had bitten him and he had scratched off the skin; he lay stupid in my arms, and seemed not to notice anything, and he had pulled the hair all out of the back of his head; They had both been two days without food.

The enlarged group of eight persons, four children and four adults, reached the Brown cabin at nightfall (Sunday, August 24). The cabin was deserted but there was food.

The next morning (Monday, August 25), the mail carrier decided to continue to New Ulm, 25 miles distance, to obtain a rescue party for the refugees; Tommy Ireland was badly wounded and Mrs. Hurd and Mrs. Eastlick and their children were exhausted. When the mail carrier got near New Ulm, he found the town deserted.[149] He returned to the Brown cabin the following day (Tuesday, August 26) and stayed in a field near the cabin overnight because he feared there were

---

[149] Charles Flandrau had ordered the town evacuated because of the damage to the buildings and the fear of another Indian attack. The inhabitants, some 2000, had left that morning for Mankato.

Indians nearby. The next day (Wednesday, August 27) he went to the cabin and told the Eastlicks, Hurds, and Tommy Ireland that there was no help available in New Ulm because it was deserted. The mail carrier told them that he would go back to Sioux Falls and try to get a rescue party from there. He set out for Sioux Falls that same day. When the mail carrier reached Sioux Falls, the town was deserted. The residents there also feared an attack by Indians and had left. The mail carrier went on to Vermilion; he abandoned his horse which was "entirely worn out, and unable to travel any further."[150] At this point the mail carrier drops from sight in the narrative.[151]

MERTON EASTLICK, CARRYING HIS BROTHER JOHNNY FROM LAKE SHETEK TO DUTCH CHARLEY'S

Fig. 9: Johnnie, Merton, and Tommy Ireland

Back at the cabin the Hurds, Eastlicks, and Tommy Ireland continued to wait for help. They also had the very real fear that Indians would find them defenseless. They even spent some nights out in a field for fear that Indians would come to the cabin. Ten days after the mail carrier left for Sioux Falls (Monday, September 1), Tommy Ireland, who had recovered from his injuries, set out for New Ulm. He arrived there at noon the next day (Tuesday, September 2). First Lieutenant Keyser describes Ireland's arrival:

> Uncle Tommy Ireland came to us a few days after we arrived there. He was the most distressed looking man I ever saw in my life. He had been hiding in the swamps for seven days and nights. He had lain in water in the deep grass. When we examined him, we found seventeen bullet holes where he had been shot by the Indians. He told me about falling in with Mrs. Eastlake (sic) and her three children (sic).[152]

Some of the townspeople had returned to New Ulm by then and there was an army unit in town under the command of Capt. Jerome Dane, Company E of the 9th Minnesota Regiment. Ireland told him of the refugees at the Brown cabin. Dane appointed a rescue party under the command of 2nd Lieutenant John R. Roberts. Just as the party was leaving at sunset, John Wright and E.G. Koch, who were from Shetek but were absent when the Indians came on August 20th, came into town and joined the soldiers. The rescue party arrived at the Brown cabin at midnight and the Hurds and Eastlick, overjoyed at being rescued, offered the soldiers a midnight snack. Everyone stayed up the rest of the night and they left the Brown cabin at sunrise on Wednesday, September 3. As they passed near Leavenworth, about three miles from the Brown cabin, they came upon the bodies of

---

[150] Bryant and Murch 1864, 161

[151] Hibschman 1901

[152] 1st Lieutenant Clark Keyser in his reminiscences says he was in charge of the rescue party and that the party left at 4:00 a.m.. (Keyser 1915, 180-181).

the Brown family, killed and mutilated by the Indians. They arrived in New Ulm at noon. The Eastlicks and the Hurds left New Ulm after resting for two days and arrived in Mankato on the 5th. Mrs. Hurd, her 3-year old son William and the unnamed infant then dropped out of the narrative. Her only other appearance is her testimony to the reparation commissions that spring.[153]

By September, 2, nearly two weeks after the attack on Shetek, all the refugees had found safety in New Ulm, St. Peter, or Mankato. Mrs. Myers had died, but the others found family and friends who had survived.

One more casualty

Joseph Gilfillan (1835-1862) was born in New York in 1835 to James and Eunice Gilfillan. In 1856 he came, apparently alone, to Minnesota and was one of the first settlers in Jamestown Township in Blue Earth County. Jamestown Township is in the northeastern portion of Blue Earth County and includes the present-day town of Madison Lake. He was unmarried and likely farmed, although the 1860 census does not indicate he was a farmer.

On August 13 he enlisted and joined Company E of the Ninth Minnesota Regiment. He went with the Company to Ft. Snelling for training, with Capt. James Dane as the commander of the company. Shortly after arriving in Ft. Snelling, they were called back to Mankato because of concern that the Winnebago would join in the US-Dakota War. The company then went to Lake Crystal and then on August 29th Capt. Dane was directed to go to New Ulm, which had been evacuated four days earlier. Company E camped in New Ulm. On September 2, when Tommy Ireland got to New Ulm with his news of the refugees, Joseph Gilfillan was in the group of fourteen men, under the command of Lieutenant John Roberts to go the Brown cabin where the refugees were hiding. Included in the group of soldiers were two civilians, John Wright and E.G. Koch. Wright and Koch had been absent when the Shetek settlers were attacked on August 20 and they wanted news of the survivors. Wright's wife and children had been taken captive and he did not know where they were.

The rescue party arrived at the cabin around midnight, September 2/3. The next morning, September 3, when the rescue party left with the Eastlicks and the Hurds, Joseph Gilfillan was delayed in mounting his horse. The others left the Brown cabin, expecting Gilfillan to catch up with them. When they were several miles from the cabin, Lieutenant Roberts was told that Gilfillan was missing and he sent three men back to search for him. They searched but did not find Gilfillan and they returned to their group. Later a farmer found Gilfillan's pocket book or diary and a part of his belt near New Ulm.

The farmer who had found Gilfillan's possessions went to New Ulm and showed Capt. Dane what he found. Dane sent a group of soldiers back to the Leavenworth area where they searched the area where Gilfillan's things were

---

[153]   One of the historical accounts (Moore 1866, pp. 55ff) has her living with her brother in La-Crosse, Wisconsin.

found. Gilfillan apparently had taken a different route when he tried to catch up with the other soldiers. His body was found on that trail. He had been shot in the chest and his head had been cut off and mutilated. The soldiers buried Gilfillan's body where they found it, returned to New Ulm, and reported his death to Capt. Dane. It was thought that the Dakota who killed him were the same ones who had killed Robert Jones. The *Mankato Semi-Weekly Record* (September 12, 1862) carried a brief article on Gilfillan, ending with, "He was a single man, and highly esteemed by his fellow-citizens." The lake near his homestead, Gilfillin Lake, was named after him. In January of 1863 a group of six soldiers was sent to bring Gilfillan's remains to Mankato where a funeral was held and his body was buried in Mankato.[154]

Postscript

Aaron Myers, whose wife died in Mankato shortly after she arrived there after fleeing from Shetek, died in Garretson, SD, on March 10, 1906, age 81. He had moved to South Dakota in 1882. Three of his children survived him, a son, Arthur, died in Salt Lake City in 1907, age 56. Louisa Myers, who was absent when Shetek was attacked, died in 1900, age 50. There are no records for Addie, born in 1861, nor of her sister, Olive, born in 1854. Fred Myers, born in 1857, died a year after the attack (1863).

Myers has this conclusion:

> Oh! You who stand by your loved ones as they taste pain on soft pillows, with every appliance of help and home comfort, think of my wife, alone in the woods, with three wounded men, and four small children, no doctor and no nurse. How could I save her, how could I reach her, was the ever prevailing thought of my mind, as the cry of the officers urging their men, the wailing of women, and the swearing of men, mingled with the fierce shout of the Indians. For years and years I have dreamed of that time, of our home, so pleasant, seemingly secure, the yard full of flowers which my wife had planted, the June sun shining as bright as my baby girl came to greet me, and then to awake and realize that I had been robbed of my wife and home, and was left with five children, the oldest only 12 years, and without a dollar or a change of clothes. But through the help of an all merciful God, I have raised all my children except one boy, who died the year after his mother, to noble manhood and womanhood, to be the stay of my declining years, and I truly believe that underneath all pain and wrong there is a power to make all things right and just, in God's good time. Some summer morning I shall meet the wife of my youth, and in the joy of that meet-

---

[154] Board of Commissioners 1891, 417; Eastlick 1864/c.1885, 40-41; Neill 1882, 574, 632; *Mankato Semi-Weekly Record*, September 6, 1862, September 12, 1862.

ing, all pain and parting will be forgotten and this summer morning cannot be far away, thank God.[155]

⧖

On July 4, 1895 there was a reunion of some of the survivors of Shetek. Harper Workman and Neil Currie invited Aaron Myers, Thomas Ireland, Lavina East-lick, Johnnie Eastlick, and Charlie Hatch to come to the town of Currie, just below Lake Shetek. David and John Burns who had been at Walnut Grove in 1862 were also invited.

The railroad had not yet reached Currie, so Lavina, Johnnie, and Tommy Ireland might have taken a wagon or carriage from Mankato. Lavina was 62 and Tommy was 83 and the wagon ride might have been tiring. They could, however, have taken the railroad through New Ulm, Sleepy Eye, and Tracy. The route from Sleepy Eye to Tracy would have followed the Shetek trail 20 miles to the south; Johnnie probably would not have recognized anything but Lavina and Tommy might have. But if they did take that route, Workman would have had to provide other transportation from Tracy to Currie. The Burns brothers came from Spring-field where they were farming, Charley Hatch, now 58, came from Huntley, Minnesota, south of Mankato. Aaron Myers at 70 years came from his home in Garretson, S.D., northeast of Sioux Falls.

Currie had a population of around 200 in 1895, but there was a hotel for them if they wished to stay over night, and perhaps Workman provided a lunch.

The newspaper account provides brief descriptions of the stories told by Lavina, Charlie, Tommy, Aaron, and the Burns' brothers.

> Today, July 9th, 1894, Ireland, Hatch, Myers, Mrs. Eastlick and Johnnie, with Neil Currie and myself, drove over this country to the points on the east side of the Lake, locating the location of the houses, route of Sioux Falls and New Ulm Trail, the place where Clark was bur-ied, Slaughter Slough, where the settlers left the wagon, where Ireland and Hatch buried the dead, where the dead Indians were found, where the bodies of Andrew Kock and John Voigt lay, and went to the graves. The Slough is in the N.E. ¼ S.3, T. 107, R. 40. The wagon was left on the knoll north of the slough, the fight was made from the south side, and the grass was taller on that side and it gave them better cover.
>
> The Trail was on the south side of the slough but they had left the trail for some reason, likely trying to avoid the Indians who were after them. Then they saw the Indians would soon overtake them they stopped the wagon and let the women and children run into the slough, the men following. When the Indians reached the wagon, they began to take the harness off of the horses, and all agree that Rhodes shot one of these Indians. Ireland claims to have killed Lean Bear in the fight though Mrs. Eastlick and Mrs. Kock say that Eastlick fired that shot.

---

[155]   Myer, Aaron. 1900, 1906. Reminiscence and Biographical Data. Typed manuscript. Shetek Collection, Brown County Museum, Brown County Historical Society, New Ulm, MN

Duley also says that he shot him. When Ireland and Hatch came back in October, 1862, they found the bodies of three Indians, two besides the one at the wagon, and that of Lean Bear, whose body is reported to have been taken to Redwood. I have so far been unable to learn on what authority.[156]

There isn't any more information on the reunion on the 4th, but they did travel the 10 miles north to where their cabins were in 1862. They could easily have identified the locations of the cabins although there were other people living there. They probably visited the mass grave near where the present day monument stands. The fence around the grave would have been the only indication of what the ground contained. Lavina would have looked at a marker-less grave of her husband and two boys; Ireland would have looked at the resting place of his wife and two young daughters; Hatch would have stood before the grave of his sister and niece; Myers would have thought about his friends and neighbors in this plot of ground. There may have been tears, but they all had 33 years to weep over the horror that happened on that warm August day. It was over and there was just a nameless fence. It would be 30 years before the monument with the names of the dead was erected.

They then went a couple miles east to Slaughter Slough. There, perhaps prompted by Workman and Currie, they talked and shared their painful stories. Johnnie had heard his mother's account but the others may have added things he didn't know. Lavina probably brought copies of her book along in case anyone was buying.

When the day was over, they left and Workman should have provided a good meal and housing if they desired.

But they had other lives now. Myers had remarried after his wife died of her wounds; Tommy Ireland had remarried, twice, and was still farming. Uncle Charlie, the Paul Revere of Shetek, found a wife and raised a family. Lavina had grandchildren from both Johnnie and her daughter, Laura; and she was planning a move to a new farm in Monticello. Myers returned to his family in South Dakota, the Burns' brothers to their farms in Springfield.

Life went on, as the cliché says, but they would always remember. The pain had dulled and the images burned into their minds may not have been as vivid, but they would never forget.

---

[156] This copy is in the Workman papers.

VI

The Eastlicks after Shetek

Lavina was a survivor. She had been driven from her home with her husband and five sons. She had endured a three-hour siege in the Wright cabin and a desperate ride across the prairie with 33 other panic-driven men, women, and children. For several hours she lay in a slough, she saw her husband killed, she was wounded in the foot, in the arm, and in her scalp. She heard and saw her friends killed. She saw her four-year-old son beaten and stabbed and her ten-year old son shot in the mouth and body. She was shot a fourth time in the back and then beaten with the stock of a gun into unconsciousness. She crawled through the charnel house of the slough coming across dead and dying men, women, and children, including her two-year-old son. Leaving her dead husband and three dead or dying sons, she crawled around on the prairie for two days and nights. Later reunited with two of her sons, she hid in a cabin for eleven days before being rescued and taken to New Ulm; she arrived in New Ulm on September 4th.

Fig. 10: Merton, Johnnie, and Lavina Eastlick, November 1862

She then was taken to Mankato where she was hospitalized and her wounds dressed; she says she stayed in the hospital for five or six weeks. There is a letter discharging her from the hospital dated October 6 from her surgeon.[157] She met some of the other survivors, Mr. Everett and Charlie Hatch, and traded stories with them. She and her sons had many visitors in Mankato; the visitors were particularly interested in seeing the two heroic boys, Merton and Johnnie. The soldiers of the 25th Wisconsin took up a collection for the family.

---

[157] Mankato Oct 6th 1862 / I do hereby certify that Mrs. Lavina Eastlick has been under my charge in Hospital at this place since the 5th day of Sept last in consequence of wounds received from Indians at Lake Shetek in the state of Minn. / W. R. McMahan, surgeon; / Wm H. Hills, Hospital Steward. (McMahan, W. R., Mankato, to Citizens, October 6, 1862. Minnesota State Archives, Auditor warrants claim records refugees, MHS, Minnesota Historical Society, St. Paul, MN.)

Lavina, being Lavina, also had a run-in with the hospital staff. When she had partially recovered, the doctor tried to send her to work in the kitchen to pay for her stay in the hospital. Refusing to do that, she was ordered out of the hospital.

She wanted to return to her parents in Ohio, but she had to go to St. Paul to obtain a pass to leave Minnesota. The first pass she received was apparently incorrect,[158] so she sought out Flandrau for a new pass which he gave her.[159] He also included a request to General Pope for a pass so she could leave the state.[160]

Making her way to General Pope's headquarters she was told to go to Governor Ramsey. She went to the Capitol, found Ramsey, and told him her story. Ramsey had read reports of Merton and Johnnie and he asked whether he could have pictures taken of her and her two sons. She agreed and stayed overnight in St. Paul.

The picture that was taken for Ramsey shows the typical family pose. A mother, sitting, holding an infant while a man—in this case a child, Merton—stands behind the woman looking over her right shoulder. Lavina looks fit, wearing a stylish cape and bonnet, showing no signs of her injuries or trauma although this must have been in late October, about two months after the attack. Johnnie also appears healthy; he stares into the camera with interest and wants to reach toward the photographer. But it is Merton's haunting look that attracts the viewer. Dark circles rim his eyes, his shoulders sag, his clothes seem ill-fitting; he appears to have lived his life and is much older than eleven. The viewer is reminded of his mother's description when she came upon the two boys in the prairie: "…now he could hardly stand alone; for he felt no fear now, and had nothing to excite him or keep up his strength. He was the poorest person I ever saw, able to stand alone."[161]

---

[158]   Mankato, Oct 3, 1862 / Mr. P. Berkey, / Dear Sir or Madam: / Mrs. Eastlick the laidie that you gave a pass at Mankato Hospital must be a mistake as regard to the place to wich she wishes to go. You gave a pass to Otonner wich is not the place for she has no friends and would be worse off their than her if she goe any where she wishes to go to this to her family where she can be taken care of. / Edwin Bradley / Provost Marshal (sic)(Bradley, Edwin, Mankato, to P. Berkey, October 3, 1862. Minnesota State Archives, Auditor warrants claim refugees, MHS, Minnesota Historical Society, St. Paul, MN.

[159]   Headquarters Ind. Exp / South Bend Oct. 4, 1862 / Mrs. Eastlick the bearer of this was wounded by the Indians at Lake Sheteck, and her husband and several children killed. The stage, Steamboat and Ferry proprietors will please pass her from Mankato to St. Paul together with her remaining children and charge to the state. The Hotel proprietors will also please assist her and children on the road. \ Chas. E. Flandrau / Col. Comdy (Flandrau, Charles, South Bend, to Major General Pope, October 5, 1862. Minnesota State Archives, Auditor warrants for claim records civilians, MHS, Minnesota Historical Society, St. Paul, MN.)

[160]   Headquarters Ind. Exp. / South Bend, Oct 5, 1862 / Maj. Gen. Pope / St. Paul / The bearer of this is Mrs. Eastlick who was wounded at Lake Sheteck, her husband and children were all killed by the Indians. She is destitute of means and wants a pass from you that will take her to Ohio free of expense. I pass her to St. Paul but can only recommend beyond the state lines. Truly your obt. Svt \ Chas. E. Flandrau Col. Cmdg. (Flandrau, Charles, South Bend, to Citizens, October 4, 1862. Minnesota State Archives, Auditor warrants claim refugees, MHS, Minnesota Historical Society, St. Paul, MN.)

[161]   Eastlick 1864, p. 32

After the picture-taking Lavina and her sons caught a stage to St. Charles. On that stage was John Stevens, a house painter from Rochester, who was looking for other things to paint. This meeting must have taken place in the third week of October.

He was interested in her story because he had started painting a panorama and he wanted to include scenes of the Dakota attacks. He offered to pay her if she would remain in Rochester so he could paint those scenes based on her descriptions. She describes their meeting:

> Next morning Mr. Bauder handed me a small sum of money, which he said he and others had contributed, and the stage agent gave me a ticket to St. Charles, so I was soon on my way. On the stage was a man named John Stevens, an artist by profession. He had learned of my misfortune, and asked me a great many questions. He had a panorama of the war nearly completed, and offered, if I would stay with him until he had painted some additional scenes of the Indian massacres, to give me the benefit of the first exhibition at Winona. He thought it would pay me well for staying. It would be about four weeks before its completion. I concluded to stay among my old neighbors, who gave me a hearty welcome.[162]

When they reached St. Charles, they met Mrs. Maria Koch who had been freed at Camp Release and was returning east. Mrs. Koch told Lavina the events that happened after the fight in the slough and her capture and rescue at Camp Release. Stevens likely listened to these stories for details to paint into the scenes of his panorama.[163] Mrs. Koch also told Lavina about Belle Duley's death (which became a scene in the panorama) and that Lavina's son Frank was still alive after the fight in the slough.[164]

---

[162]   Eastlick 1864, p. 49; the "old neighbors" may have been people the Eastlicks knew from their brief stay in Olmsted County in 1857.

[163]   There is a letter that suggests Lavina did more than tell the story of Shetek. In a letter written by John Eastlick, the son of Johnnie (6/18/48, Olmsted County Historical Society Archives), says "My grandmother used to tell us kids about the panorama made by John Stevens, how she posed for pictures and drawings and how he showed her with a white collar. As I remember, she said it was certainly a far fetched sketch of the actual conditions of those who escaped the massacre."

[164]   Frank Eastlick, the ten-year old son of John and Lavina, is the lost child of Shetek. He was severely wounded in the Slough, shot in the mouth, abdomen, and leg. His body, however, was never found. The Shetek Monument notes that a fifteenth victim unnamed on the monument, is also buried in this common grave, but it is not the body of Frank. In the first burial of the bodies in October 1862, this body was incorrectly identified as Frank Eastlick, but it was realized at the second internment (October 1863) that the remains were of an older child, who remains unknown. Forrest (Forrest, Robert and J. D. Weber, compilers. n.d. *A History of Murray County from 1833 to 1950. Sections of an unpublished history.* Shetek Documents, Murray County Historical Society, Slayton, MN.) recounts what is believed to have happened to Frank. Joe LeBeau (or the more well-known Joe LaFramboise), a half-breed trapper had been wounded in the Conflict and he made his way to Shetek. He arrived there on August 24 (Workman 1924, 54). In the Smith cabin he found a boy, presumably Frank, severely wounded in the mouth. The boy had survived on some food he found in the house. LeBeau remained with the boy over several weeks at the lake. He then took the boy west to the Missouri River. When LeBeau

Mrs. Koch urged Lavina to return to Mankato and testify against the Dakota who had been jailed in Mankato after being transported form the Lower Sioux Agency. Lavina went to Rochester instead and stayed there for a week, helping Stevens with the panorama. She then went to Mankato, taking Merton and Johnnie, to inquire about the reparations she had applied for. She visited with William Everett who was recovering from his wounds in the hospital. She also went to Camp Lincoln near Mankato, where the condemned Dakota were being held. She observed their conditions and concluded,

> The prisoners seemingly enjoying life much better than they deserved, some sleeping, some smoking, some eating, and some playing cards. It made my blood boil, to see them so merry, after their hellish deeds. I felt as if I could see them butchered, one and all, and no one, who has suffered what we settlers have, from their ferocity, can entertain any milder feelings toward them.[165]

Being Lavina, she got into an argument with the person (Buck) handling her reparations claim and hired another, whose rate was smaller.[166] The first burial

---

returned to Minnesota in 1873 he spoke with Myers at the State Fair in St. Paul. In answer to a question from Myers, LeBeau said that he had taken the boy to Dakota Territory, but he did not know what became of him. In the Aaron Myers's letter to Neil Currie (Workman 1924, 112) Myers repeated the story of LeBeau relating how he found Frank in the Smith cabin. The burial party that came to the lake in October 1862 reported that there were indications that a child had lived there for some time. The presumed occupant had done housework and collected food from the garden. It wasn't clear how the burial party deduced it was a child who had lived there. There was also a rumor that the child had stayed there for three months. But the fate of Frank Eastlick remains unknown. Lavina at first believed, based on the story that Mrs. Koch told her, that Frank was alive. In her interview with the *Grant County Herald* and in her book, she says that Frank is alive. There is no indication that she changed her mind over the years. There is the possibility that he lived out his life on the prairie, perhaps never knowing what became of his parents. Recently, it is said that a descendant of his lives in California and attended a reunion at Lake Shetek. There is also a family story, undocumented, that an Eastlick relative said that her father used to talk about a relative named Frank Eastlick who had the nickname of Hambone Eastlick. He was called Hambone because of his disfigured mouth. His age and the disfigured mouth lead some researchers to believe that Frank "Hambone" Eastlick was in fact Frank Eastlick. These stories suggest that Lavina abandoned her children; an example of that conclusion is in a recently published history of Minnesota. Wingerd, the author, dismisses Lavina Eastlick's heroism and states that "other survivor accounts [none indicated] mention [Lavina Eastlick] in much less flattering terms as coldheartedly abandoning anyone who slows her flight, including her children" (Mary Lethert Wingerd, 2010. *North County: The Making of Minnesota*. Minneapolis, University of Minnesota Press, page 400, footnote 11). This evaluation of Lavina Eastlick appears to be an unsupported conclusion by Wingerd.

165   Eastlick 1864, p. 54

166   Her new representative was David Wilcox. Persons who suffered loss in the 1862 Dakota War were allowed to file depredation claims for their loss and suffering. In filing the claim the claimant had to document the loss and provide affidavits from others who would support the loss. They could also seek emergency funds for travel, lodging, or other needs. In these cases they may have been given funds, vouchers, or requests for special consideration. (See Bakeman, Mary, compiler. (2001) *Index to Claimants for Depredations Following the Dakota War of 1862*. Roseville, MN: Park Genealogical Books, and Bakeman, Mary, compiler. (2009) *Emergency Aid for the Suffers from the Dakota Conflict*, Vol 5 1862-1863. Roseville, MN: Park Genealogical Books.) Lavina Eastlick filed depredation claims for $540. In today's money using the Consumer Price

Fig. 11: John Stevens

party had returned from Shetek and they brought with them her husband's rifles. She gave one of the rifles to Tommy Ireland and kept the other as a memento of her husband.

She then went back to Stevens's home in Rochester. He convinced her to leave Merton with him; he said he would bring Merton to her in Wisconsin in a couple of weeks. She agreed and continued her journey to St. Charles, where she met another Shetek survivor, Aaron Myers. They also traded stories; Myers filled her in on the details of the first group to flee Shetek. After another small disagreement over the stage coach fare, she went on to Winona, LaCrosse, Madison (by rail), Boscobal, and Lancaster.[167]

From Lancaster she went to her brother's home near Ellenboro. In Lancaster she was asked by the editor of the local newspaper to tell her story.

Merton was returned to Lavina in Lancaster and later she went on to her parents' home in Ohio. She remained there during the summer of 1863. In the fall she returned to Lancaster, and during the winter she wrote her account.

Lavina Eastlick returned to Minnesota in 1865. Her book was apparently selling, and after a brief stay in Hennepin County, she moved to Mankato with her sons, Merton and Johnnie. Lavina bought land in Mankato Township on July 23, 1867 from George Maynard. The land included the SE ¼ of the SE ¼ in section 22, T108N R26W, 40 acres and the SW ¼ of the SW ¼ of section 23, T108N R26W, 55 acres. The total price appears to have been $890. She said she bought it very cheap with money she had received in reparations. The land in the 1879 plat map and the current topological map show a lake that includes most of those 80 acres. (See Plate 18). The plat map names the lake as N. Goster Lake. Today's maps do not have it named. It doesn't appear to be tillable land.

Index (see Samuel H. Williamson, "Seven Ways to Compute the Relative Value of a U.S. Dollar Amount, 1774 to present," *Measuring Worth,* April 2010.) that would be $12,100. She also received assistance for passage to Winona for herself and her two children ($1.00/$22.00), stage coach passage from St. Charles to Winona ($7.00/$154.00), lodging for herself and her two children ($3.00/$66.00), a woolen shawl for her ($4.00/$88.00), and she was given a written request asking "hotel proprietors, please assist." The moneys for these claims and for the emergency assistance were taken from the Dakota annuity funds that Congress confiscated when they abrogated all Dakota treaties in March 1863.

[167] She gives these towns in this order in her narrative, but it appears strange because both Boscobal and Lancaster are in southwestern Wisconsin, south west of Madison, which would required her to go back west after getting to Madison. Perhaps the trains and coaches required that roundabout route to Lancaster.

There was a William Ireland who owned land in the northern part of the same quarter sections. This seems to have been a relative of Tommy Ireland, the Eastlick's friend. Tommy Ireland was in Mankato at this time. He had survived the journey from Shetek and got to New Ulm. He then went to Mankato and remained there until he recovered from his wounds. He was in Mankato at the time of the executions on December 26, 1862. The *Mankato Independent* (December 26, 1862) carried a brief notice that he visited the log prison where the 38 condemned Dakota were kept and he "recognized the Indian who had shot him at Lake Shetek. He thereupon requested that his own evidence be taken in an official form. Col. Miller agreed that it should be done on Saturday of this week, and Dr. Williamson has consented to stay over and act as interpreter."

Later Ireland placed his two surviving daughters, Rosanna (8) and Ellen Nellie (6) up for adoption. They had been taken captive at Shetek and later freed in South Dakota. There were reunited with their father in Fort Dodge, Iowa, in January 1863. Ellen Nellie was adopted by Mr. and Mrs. R. K. Boyd, her mother's relatives. Boyd had fought at Birch Coulee. Roseanne (8) was also adopted by her mother's relatives in Montana. Ellen later married A. C. Hotaling and lived in Mankato until her death in 1946.[168] Rosanna married a Van Alstone; she died in 1936 in Missoula. Montana.

Tommy Ireland, 50 years old, went briefly to Illinois, returned to Minnesota in 1866, married a widow named Sally Haddock, and returned to Shetek living near the Hurd cabin. After Sally died in 1882, he returned to Mankato and married again (1885) to Sophia Waters. When he was interviewed in 1893, at age 81 Workman described him as a tall man, 6'3" and a good talker.

The ownership and mortgaging of Lavina's land in the following years also provides some insights into Lavina's situation. In 1873 Lavina mortgaged one of the pieces of land to William Duley. She also mortgaged the other section of land to John Diamond in 1875 and paid off the mortgage in 1876.[169] On May 3, 1901, she paid the mortgage she had with William Duley and then sold the land to Gottfried Strobel on May 27, 1901, retaining a mortgage on the property until 1907 when Strobel paid off the mortgage.

Henry Smith

On the 1879 plat map the land that Lavina bought in Mankato is shown as owned L[avina] Smith. On March 31, 1865, Lavina married Henry Watson Smith and she apparently used her married name when she purchased the land. The witnesses at the wedding were Joseph (William?) Duley and Laura Duley. The minister was listed as Thomas Day, apparently not a relative of Lavina. William and Laura Duley had been neighbors of the Eastlick family in Shetek. Mrs. Duley was one of the captives who were eventually freed in South Dakota. They

---

[168] Ellen apparently was the last living survivor of Shetek.

[169] Lavina's fortunes paralleled the country. The Panic of 1873 was followed by several years of depression.

were living in the Mankato area and it would be natural for them to attend and witness Lavina's marriage to another survivor of Shetek.

Henry Smith and his wife Sophia had come to Shetek in 1855, one of the first of the settlers in that area. Smith Lake on the southern part of Lake Shetek was named after him and it was there that he had his cabin. At the time of the attack on Shetek in August 1862, he and his wife had also been warned by Charlie Hatch that the Dakota Indians were killing the settlers and they had fled to the Wright cabin. Later when the fleeing settlers made their desperate run to Slaughter Slough, Henry Smith kept on running, despite the cries of his wife that he not desert her. He continued running, however, to Walnut Grove where he warned some settlers, and then he continued on to New Ulm. Sophia Smith was wounded in the initial shooting. Later, when the women and children came out of the Slough, she was shot again and died.

Whatever Smith did at Shetek, he later joined the army. He was mustered in on October 11, 1862, two months after Shetek. He joined the first Regiment of Mounted Rangers, Company B. The regiment was formed in the fall of 1862 to meet the need for cavalry during the Dakota War. During the winter of 1862/63 the regiment patroled the frontier and they were stationed at some of the forts constructed in central Minnesota. In 1863, the regiment under Colonel McPhail was part of the Sibley expedition to the Dakota Territory in pursuit of the Dakota who left Minnesota. Smith may have fought in the Battle of Big Mound in July 1863. They returned to Minnesota in the fall of 1863 and Smith was mustered out on November 9, 1863.[170]

The wedding of Henry and Lavina was likely a small ceremony and one cannot help but wonder about the reception after the wedding. Laura Duley, who saw her four-year old and her 10-year old son killed in the slough, who endured a horrific four-month captivity with her other three children, sits quietly drinking tea. She was likely suffering from the mental and emotional trauma that later led to her being institutionalized in a mental hospital. William Duley was only slightly wounded at Shetek and he got back to New Ulm safely. One can hear Duley regale the guests with stories of his heroism, how he designed the gallows at Mankato (which he didn't but said he did), and how he cut the rope that hung the 38 Dakota (which he did). Smith talks about how he heroically warned settlers as he fled from his wife at Shetek. Merton Eastlick who was now 14 and Johnnie, almost four, were probably too polite to say anything.

The kind of baggage that both Lavina and Henry Smith brought to the wedding did not bode well for the marriage to be a life-long union. And it wasn't. One month later, Lavina walked out (Henry said) and 19 months later (January 24, 1867) they were divorced.

Transcripts of divorce proceedings sometimes give insights into the life and activities of the husband and wife as they debate why a marriage is failing. (The complete divorce transcript is in Appendix A.) In the transcript, James Savage,

---

[170] Board of Commissioners, ed. 1891. *Minnesota in the Civil and Indian Wars 1861-1865. Vol. 1,* St. Paul, MN: Pioneer Press, p. 519ff.

a witness for the plaintiff (Henry Smith) said that for a period of nine weeks Lavina was absent, touring southern Minnesota, apparently to sell her book. During that time she left her son, probably Johnnie, with the Savage family. Henry Smith testified that "although he always conducted himself … as a father and dutiful husband," the defendant, disregarding her "duties as a wife has willfully deserted and has been willfully absent from the plaintiff for the time of one year next preceding the filing of this complaint."[171]

Lavina denied the accusations and said her ten week absence was for "business mutually beneficial to both parties" and both had agreed to her absence. In addition, Lavina testified that it was Henry Smith who left for 10 months to visit relatives in Connecticut and that he did not furnish "clothing, food, or sustenance of any kind whatsoever." She further alleged that Smith did not use "language toward the defendant in accordance with common decency as a husband ought to do." Lavina did admit, however, that she and her husband had "tempers and dispositions [that were] somewhat uncongenial," but that again was his fault. Lavina said the divorce should not be granted, but if it was granted, the court should direct Smith to turn over to her the proportion of his property allowed by law.

Henry Smith denied all her claims and allegations. It was she who "left during hoeing and just before haying" and he left to visit his relatives in Connecticut because he became tired of performing "the cooking and house work for a period of six to eight weeks." Besides, he was gone during the winter months, not at harvest time. He disagreed with Lavina's testimony about his assets and said that he was worth only $1800 and she was worth $1500 and she "still has on hand a large amount of books or pamphlets." Henry further denied that "he had been peevish or ill-natured toward her."

The judge, probably without too much difficulty, realized that Lavina and Henry were not meant for each other, and he declared the marriage was dissolved on January 24, 1867. Lavina was not awarded any money and Henry Watson Smith disappears from the picture.

Lavina returned to farming, housekeeping, and selling her book. Merton would have been 15 and able to help with the farming. He was also learning to be a carpenter because he built a small frame house for Lavina in the summer of 1867 and in the next summer he put on an addition with a kitchen, two bedrooms, and a buttery (storeroom/pantry). Merton also worked as a carpenter to supplement the income from the farm. Lavina probably continued to sell her book in southern Minnesota. Lavina observed that they now had a "comfortable living."

Solomon Pettibone

But to even "better her condition," on November 17, 1870 Lavina married Solomon Pettibone. The wedding took place in her home, with Leicester Day, Lavina's brother, as a witness. At the time of the marriage Solomon was living in Elysian, 12 miles east of Mankato. Solomon is a bit of a puzzle because there

---

[171] The Minnesota State Census of June 1, 1865, shows Henry Smith as living alone.

is very little information on him. Census records and Laura's birth certificate indicate that he had been born around 1809 in either Michigan or Connecticut. That would have made him 60 years old when he became Lavina's third husband (Lavina would have been 37). He is listed as a farmer (sometimes painter) and he was living with the family of Delos (37) and Jerusha (33) Fish. Jerusha apparently was his niece, the daughter of Erastus Pettibone, a brother of Solomon. The Pettibone family came from Ohio and some members of the larger family were quite prominent, including a congressman and an owner of a manufacturing plant.

The Fish family also provides a upstream connection to Ross Irish and Mert Fish, two men who provided the verification papers in the 1962 printing of Lavina's book. Delos and Jerusha Fish had several children, one of whom was Alice (1866?-1918?) born in Elysian. Alice married Mortimer/Mert Irish in Genoa, Nebraska, in 1902(?). Their son was Ross Irish who compiled the affidavits and pictures for the book and which are included in the 1962 printing in the front and back of the book. Mert Fish, who signed the Platte, Nebraska, affidavit, was the brother of Alice. Ross Irish is identified as the nephew of Lavina; if the above genealogy is correct, he would have been the great nephew (or great-great nephew) of Lavina. Descendants of the Fish and Irish families still live in the Genoa/Columbus area in east central Nebraska. And the Irish family seems to appear in both Monticello and Alberta.

Even more of a mystery is what happened to Solomon. Lavina says in February 1871 he unexpectedly left Mankato and went to visit his sister in Ohio. After a brief visit, he left his sister's home and disappeared. Lavina never heard from him again and there are no available documents that indicate his fate or whereabouts. Lavina later assumed (or knew) that he was dead.

More marriages

Six months after Solomon left, on August 27, 1871, Laura Jennie Pettibone was born. Her birth certificate shows Solomon, age 60 as her father (deceased) and Lavina Day (40) as her mother. Solomon's occupation is listed as "painter" and Lavina is a housewife.[172]

Merton, now 22, seemed to have moved out around this time. The 1871-72 Mankato City Directory lists him as a boarder near Hickory and Walnut streets in Mankato and shows his occupation as a laborer. Johnnie, 10, took care of his half-sister, Laura, while Lavina farmed with the help of her neighbors.

Early in 1873 Merton moved again, this time to Rochester. There he operated a rag store and sold used clothing and met a young lady, Mary Ann Alexander. Things seemed to go well because Merton and Mary were married on August 19, 1873. Lavina said that Merton and Mary invited her to live with them, but Lavina, as she later would several other times, refused because she "didn't want to

---

[172] The birth certificate on record at the Blue Earth Country records is not the original. The birth record is an affidavit by John Eastlick, Laura's half brother, in 1941. He affirmed that the date and place of Laura's birth were correct. The absence of the original birth certificate is described as the "neglect of the attending physician."

be a burden." Her refusal could also be an example of that strong sense of independence that she had.

Mary Alexander was the second eldest child of Joseph (1820-1897) and Hannah (1822-1895) Alexander. Joseph and Hannah and their eldest son had emigrated from England in the 1850s and settled in Watertown, Wisconsin. In the early 1860s they had moved to Rochester where Joseph worked at or managed a woolen mill. Mary had been born in 1850. Eventually there were nine children in the family, including Joseph Jr. Descendants of the Alexander family still live in the Rochester area.

At this time Merton also renewed his acquaintance with John Stevens, the artist who painted the Shetek panorama and Merton had served as a sort of exhibit during the showings of the panorama in 1862/63. Stevens convinced Merton to again join him on a tour to show the panorama in the fall of 1873 in the towns of Iowa and Wisconsin. The 18th century was a time of panoramas. These panoramas could be one large painting that illustrated a particular scene, such as the Mississippi River or a battle, or a series of paintings that showed an event. Stevens did some five versions of a series of panels that featured events of the 1862 Dakota War. It apparently was a profitable venture. Lavina and other survivors of Shetek furnished Stevens with the stories that made up the panels.

The tour in the fall of 1873 was Steven's third version of his panorama. This version was a "diaphanous painting," a technique in which scenes were painted on a translucent cloth that allowed lanterns to be positioned behind the panels to illuminate them. The effect was said to be stunning, particularly because Stevens often used a lot of bright red paint. This 1873 version had 36 panels, half of them showed scenes from Shetek. Each panel was about six feet wide and five feet high. The 36 panels were painted on one piece of cloth, 222 feet long.[173] Stevens used a frame that had dowels on top and on the bottom of a wooden frame. A crank was on the lower dowel and as a helper turned the crank, each panel was rolled into view. Lanterns behind the frame illuminated the panels. There was a written script for another helper to read to the audience as each panel was revealed. Stevens also constructed a special wagon that enclosed the panorama and its frame. When the tour reached a town and the audience had gathered—and the 25 cent admission had been collected, the wagon sides were removed, the lanterns lit, the person with the script and the cranker ready to go, and the 19th century IMAX began. Merton had done this tour 10 years previously with one of Stevens early versions. At that time and probably

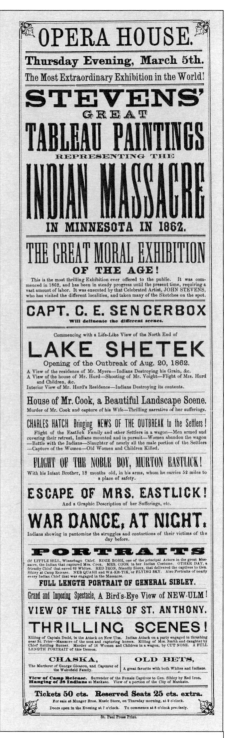

Fig. 12: Playbill for the Stevens' Panorama

---

173   The curator of the Gilcrease Museum (where this version of the panorama is currently stored) describes the cloth as similar to cheap calico. (Personal communication, 7/2011)

Fig. 13: Mechanism to operate the Stevens Panorama

also in the 1873 tour Merton provided additional commentary; he had been there, after all. The brochure advertising the tour said that "one-half of this exhibition was presented to Merton Eastlick to help support his mother, little brother and himself"—probably after expenses were deducted. Joe Alexander Jr., who cranked the panorama, is not mentioned in the advertisement, but we can assume that Merton gave his brother-in-law something.[174] The tour returned to Rochester in the spring of 1874, just in time for the birth of Merton and Mary's first child, William Merton Eastlick, on May 23, 1874. Stevens considered the tour a success but when he asked Merton to go on tour the following fall, Merton declined. Mary probably convinced Merton that a father should stay at home.

Lavina now had a grandson, her first. Travel between Mankato and Rochester had improved considerably since the coming of the railroad between the two cities in 1868. Lavina was tight with her money, but the family must have gotten together in the summer and fall.

Merton wrote his mother in the summer of 1875 that he had a severe cold, but it did not seem serious. But on November 5th Lavina got a telegraph from Mary saying that Lavina should come to Rochester because Merton was dying. Lavina arrived there the following afternoon, but Merton was already dead. Lavina was always convinced that Merton died because of the terrible suffering he had endured in his flight from Shetek.[175]

Merton was buried the next day in Oakwood Cemetery in Rochester. Lavina, Mary, and little William were there and it is probable that the Alexander family, Johnnie, and Laura, and perhaps even John Stevens attended the funeral. As they stood at the grave, Lavina wrote that she bemoaned the lack of a stone or monument for the "hero of Shetek." She also suggested that a rich man's son would have had a monument, perhaps one raised by the state to memorialize the hero.

As to whether the death of Merton went unnoticed as Lavina suggests, the *Rochester Post* (November 13, 1875) published two articles on the "Death of a Historic Character—the Boy Hero of the Sioux Massacre." The articles included an obituary and another article gave a summary of the events at Shetek and Merton's heroism in carrying his brother.

Lavina was careful about spending her money. She had several confrontations in 1862 and 1863 over what she thought were excessive charges by persons who provided her with transportation, lodging, and help with her reparations claim.

---

[174] Joe also operated the crank in 1912, the 50th anniversary of the Dakota war. At a ceremony in Rochester the Stevens panorama that had been found in Winona was shown to a special audience. Joe was 60 years old and probably smiling broadly as he again cranked the panorama.

[175] *The Rochester Post* (November 13, 1875) said Merton "caught cold from overwork in plastering a house that he was building, which resulted in typhoid fever of which he died."

The matter of money also came up in the divorce proceedings with Henry Smith. A widow in the 19th century who tried to raise children would often be in a desperate financial situation; that is why so many remarried. But Lavina does describe the previous two years as a "comfortable living," her book sales brought in some income, and she did have a working farm with helpful neighbors. Certainly there were also other friends, such as the Irelands and even Stevens, and a family such as the Alexanders who could have contributed to some type of modest grave marker. Her grief at the grave site is real and poignant as she tries to come to terms with the death of yet another son, her fourth. But her lament that someone else should have provided the gravestone has a strange sound.[176]

There is no record of Mary Ann remarrying. She lived for 57 more years, dying in Rochester on September 20, 1933 at the age of 82. She was buried in a different part of Oakwood Cemetery. William Merton, their son, married Elizabeth Margaret Bahmer in Winona on November 26, 1896. The couple lived in Rochester and had two children, Wray (1897-1972) and Blanche (1898-1994). Both of these Eastlicks married and had children, some of these children as well as their progeny still live in the Rochester area.

Lavina, Laura, and Johnnie returned to Mankato. Things were quiet for several years, although Lavina had to rebuild her house because it burned down in 1883. Johnnie had hired out so Lavina hauled the stone, mixed lime and sand to make mortar for plastering the walls, and laid the flooring of her house. She took pride in what she accomplished and asserted that "I am very determined to accomplish what I undertake."

In 1885 Johnnie was 24 and working away from home. In the Mankato Directory he is listed as a farmer in 1888, but there isn't any indication that he owned land; a later census located Johnnie as living in ward 3 of Mankato. A photograph at that time shows John Eastlick operating what may be a custom threshing machine (Fig. 15). He also met a young lady, Margretha (Margaret/Maggie) McKee of St. Peter.

Maggie had been born on November 27, 1864 in St. Peter where her father farmed in Traverse Township. She had a brother John, born in 1863. Her father, John William, had been born in New York in 1834. He moved to the St. Peter area sometime in the 1850s, where he met and married Marianna

Fig. 14: Monument to Merton Eastlick, Olmsted County

---

[176] Lavina, did, in a sense, get her marker. In 1962 at the 100th anniversary of the Dakota War, the Olmsted County Historical Society donated a fine stone marker for Merton's grave. The marker was first proposed by Burt Eaton in 1912 when he showed the rediscovered Stephens' panorama. The marker identifies Merton as the "Boy Hero of the Indian Massacre of 1862." This Rochester version of the panorama is currently in storage at the Minnesota Historical Society. It is not available for viewing.

Fig. 15: John Eastlick in Mankato
The exact identiy of this photo remains unclear.

Walter on May 1, 1862. Marianne had been born May 21, 1845 in Alsace, France, and immigrated to the U.S. when she was 10.

On February 23, 1864 John William McKee was mustered into D Company of the 9th Minnesota Regiment. He was taken prisoner in a skirmish in Mississippi and sent to the notorious Andersonville Prison in Georgia.[177] He died there on October 30, 1864. Maggie was born in St. Peter one month later. Perhaps the tragedies of having lost a father in Maggie's case before she was born and in Johnnie's case when he was an infant gave Johnnie and Maggie something in common that brought them together. They were married on September 1, 1885 in Mankato.[178]

Soon Lavina had more grandchildren. William Frank Eastlick was born November 14, 1888 and two years later, July 7, 1890 Henry (Harry) George Eastlick was born. It was about this time that Lavina completed the Appendix for a new printing of her book by the *Mankato Free Press* in 1890. At the close of that Appendix she notes that she is living alone with Laura, now 19. She again asserts that although Johnnie and Maggie invited her to live with them, she does not want to burden them. Johnnie was still living in Mankato, Ward 3, with his growing family. She would rather "live and care for myself, and daughter, as long as I can." She did like her independence.

Soon after, the good friend of the Eastlicks, Tommy Ireland, died in Mankato on August 8, 1897, at the age of 85 in Mankato. The *Mankato Free Press* carried his obituary:

> Thos. Ireland, One of the Old Settlers Succumbs to Old Age. He was there during the Indian troubles and received numerous wounds.
> Thos. Ireland, well known to all old settlers of Blue Earth county, died yesterday from the effects of old age, being 85 years old on the 12th of March last. He has been in a feeble condition for some time back, and his death was not unexpected. Mr. Ireland took a prominent

---

[177] One of the strange coincidences that make a historian's day is that Henry Wirz, the commandant of Andersonville, in his trial after the Civil War made a list of witnesses that he believed would testify to his humane treatment of the Northern prisoners, and he included the name of A. A. Eastlick from Michigan. There is no indication that he was related to the Eastlicks in Minnesota. Wirz was convicted of war crimes and hung.

[178] Maggie's mother, Marianne, remarried in 1866 to Theodore Fitterer of Mankato and they had a child, Maria. Descendants of Maria and of John McKee Jr. probably still live in the Mankato and Bemidji areas of Minnesota. Marianne died on January 28, 1877 and is buried in Calvary Cemetery in Mankato.

part in the defense against the Indians in the early sixties, and during the war received some eighteen wounds from the red skins. Several reminiscences of his experiences have been published in these columns during the past two or three years. Of late years Mr. Ireland has resided in Tincomville, in the southern part of the city. The funeral will be held at the Tivola schoolhouse tomorrow at 10:30 o'clock. (*Mankato Free Press Daily,* August 9, 1897)

Fig. 16: Thomas Ireland

The McDonnells

In the mid-19th century large numbers of emigrants left Nova Scotia because of a downturn in the economy. The ship building industry had declined and trade had fallen off because of the Civil War in the U.S. Nova Scotia had joined the Dominion of Canada in 1867, a decision that was opposed by some Nova Scotians. Some of the Scottish people in Nova Scotia whose parents had immigrated in the early part of the century no longer saw it as the New Scotland and decided to leave.

Two of those Scottish families who came to the United States were the McDonnells and the Freemans.[179] The two families were the Alexander Urkhard McDonnell family and the William Freeman family. Alexander McDonnell's father, also named Alexander, was born in Scotland in the late 18th century and had emigrated to Nova Scotia as a young man and later married there. Alexander Urkhard, his son, was born in Lunenberg County, Nova Scotia on January 15, 1842. He married Lucy Maria Freeman in the late 1860s. Three sons, Clark, Angus, and Aubrey were born in Nova Scotia. But in 1882 Alexander and his family, and his wife's family, the Freemans, left Nova Scotia, perhaps because he saw better prospects in the United States. The Freeman family consisted of his wife's father, LeRoy, mother Caroline, and brothers Walter and Herbart. After leaving Nova Scotia the Freemans went to the Minneapolis area in Minnesota and the McDonnells went to Wright County, Minnesota, settling just east of the present town of Monticello. The McDonnell family included Alexander, 40 (born 15 Jan 1842), his wife Lucy, 38 (born 1846), sons Clark, 12 (born 19 May 1870),

---

[179] Working through the variant spellings and pronunciations of Scottish names approaches the challenges that German names present when they are transplanted to the U.S. The McDonnell name has several spellings and pronunciations. An account in the history of Lougheed by a family member illustrates this challenge: "I will explain the two different spellings of our name—the 'Mc' and the 'Mac.' It seems that the Scots did many mystifying things, and one was the altering of surnames over the winning and losing of battles or over religious differences. It was common to have one branch of the family on each side of the hill decide to have different surnames after an argument. However, ours was destined when my birth was registered by some doughty Scot in the registration office who figured I should be 'Mac.'" [Lougheed Women's Institute. 1972. *Verdant Valleys In and Around Lougheed.* Lougheed, Alberta: Lougheed Women's Institute. p. 224] At times the name of this family is also recorded as "MacDonald" or "McDonald" because that is the way the name was heard by a census taker, which leads to how the name should be pronounced. In Canada, some members of the family insist on a pronunciation with an accent on the third syllable: McDonNELL. Others are less insistent and allow a second syllable accent, McDONnell, which is very close in sound to McDonald. In consideration of the purists in Canada, the name used here is always spelled McDonnell because that is how Alexander Urkhard McDonnell signed his name, but the reader can choose her or his own pronunciation.

Angus, 10 (born 31 Mar 1872), and Aubrey, 6 (born 03 Mar 1876). The land that Alexander purchased (or at first rented) appeared to have been about a quarter mile south of the Mississippi River.[180] The land was in section 16 of Monticello Township, Wright County. (See Plate 19.)[181] Today Wright County Road 39 passes just north between the land and the Mississippi, perhaps a hundred yards from the river. The bluffs of the river are relatively low in this area and it is currently farmed; there are also housing developments moving out from the city of Monticello. In the 19th century the land would likely have been covered with trees, which may have made the land more valuable because the timber could be cut and transported down the Mississippi to one of the many saw mills on the river. The 1885 Minnesota State Census has Alexander, Lucy, Clark, Angus, and Aubrey living on the farm. A year after the census Ella McDonnell was born on June 7, 1886. Two years later William Freeman McDonnell was born (July 9, 1888).[182]

But in the 1895 Minnesota State Census, Angus, now 23, is not with his family in Wright County.[183] He is in Blue Earth County, on Lavina Eastlick's farm and living in her home with his wife, Laura. Somehow those two found each other because on March 21, 1895 Laura, and Angus McDonnell were married in Mankato, perhaps in Lavina's home. Angus is listed as a farmer and he could have been farming Lavina's land. The census data also says that Angus had been living in Minnesota since 1883 (which fits the immigration date) and in the census enumeration district for three months, which at the time the census was taken would be his and Laura's wedding. There is no indication that the Angus's family or the Freeman family ever lived in Blue Earth County and Lavina did not move out of the Mankato area until 1901. Laura had joined the Seventh Day Adventist Church in 1893. Lavina, her mother, had a religious experience in 1886 and joined the Adventists in 1894. Angus appears to have become a Seventh Day Adventist after his marriage. There is no indication that the Eastlick and McDonnell families were previously connected or that there were some common friends between the families. They were of different cultures; the Eastlicks had been in the States since before the Revolutionary War. But somehow Angus and Laura met; one thinks of a church box luncheon halfway in Hutchinson.

---

180   This location is based on a land record in which Angus purchased a parcel of land from his father in 1900.

181   Alex McDonnell also owned 120 acres in the east ½ of the east ½ of the NW ¼ and the west ½ of the NE ¼ in section 20 (Twnshp 121, R 24). The railroad tracks of the St. Paul Minneapolis and Manitoba Railroad ran through his land. In 1889 a fire started, presumably from the engine of the train, and burned McDonnell's land and 47 tons of hay and 55 rods of fence. He sued the railroad for damages. A jury heard the case and awarded him $643. The railroad tracks no longer exist.

182   One of the most informative of the federal censuses, 1890, which included middle names and additional information was almost totally destroyed in a fire in the Department of Commerce Building in Washington, D.C. in 1922. Only a few fragments were salvaged, one sheet on one family in Wight County was among the fragments. That "missing census" has stymied researchers ever since.

183   There is an Angus McDonnell living in St. Paul in 1890 and 1891, as indicated in the St. Paul City Directory. This may be the Angus from Wright County, but there is no proof.

Monticello

Angus did not stay long in Blue Earth County, but he did stay long enough for Donald, their first son, to be born on August 5, 1897. Shortly after that he and Laura moved to Monticello, probably in 1900, when, according to land records (October 8), he bought 40 acres of land from his father and mother. The 1900 census does not show Laura, Angus, or Lavina in Blue Earth County but Angus and Laura are in Wright County. They are, in fact, living, with Donald their son, next door to Angus's parents, Alexander and Lucy, and Ella and William, Angus's brother and sister.

There is no indication where Lavina was in 1900. She may have been with Johnnie, who was in Mankato. He is still living in Ward 3 of Mankato and now he is listed as a teamster. John and his family moved to Monticello in 1901 where he purchased 83 acres in section 16 in Monticello Township, the same section where Alexander and Angus had their farms.[184] (See Plate 19.) Lavina sold her land in Mankato 1901 and likely moved to Monticello at that time (or when Laura and Angus moved) and purchased a small farm of 10 acres also in section 16. The Minnesota State Census of 1905 has them all neighbors (except Johnnie and his family who aren't in the 1905 census). First, Alexander, Lucy, Ella, and William, in the next house is Caroline Freeman, then Angus, Laura, Donald, and Edna, then Lavina. It was at this time that Lavina changed her name back to East-lick. The state census does not indicate separate house-holds, only a listing of names. They all are on RFD 2, so there is no distinction in address.

It is in the 1905 census that the daughter of An-gus and Laura, Edna Grace McDonnell, appears. The records, including her tombstone, indicate she was born in 1903, but the accounts of Edna, both printed[185] and oral, state that she was adopted. One account has her being born in Mankato but that would mean that Angus and Laura returned to Mankato where they ad-opted her and brought her to their new home in Mon-ticello. There are no records of her adoption in Mankato nor in Wright County nor in Hennipin County. Nor is there any indication what her birth name was.

The 1905 Minnesota Census provides an interesting picture of the extended McDonnell/Freeman/Eastlick family (See Plate 20). In section 16 near the Missis-sippi River there was Alexander McDonald (62), his wife, Lucy (58), daughter Ella (19), son William (16).

Fig. 17: Laura, Lavina, Donald
Based on Donald's apparent age, this photo was taken around 1898 likely in Mankato.

---

[184]   Although the land records are not clear, John's obituary has him coming to Monticello in 1901; a plat map from 1916 shows the 80 acres to be in NE ¼ of Section 17.

[185]   Lougheed Women's Institute. 1972. op. cit.

Fig. 18: Logging operations

Fig. 19: John Eastlick's Children
Picture taken c. 1910: Merton 1894-1948, Cora
1898-1967, Henry 1890-1946

Next there was Caroline Freeman (85), mother of Lucy. Then there was the son of Alexander, Angus McDonnell (33) and his wife Laura (33) and their son Donald (7) and daughter Edna (2), and finally, Laura's mother, Lavina Eastlick (72). Those ten people lived on adjoining land. (See Plate 19.) Strangely intriguing was another neighbor, Charles Irish and his wife and six children. The Irish family went to Alberta with the McDonnells in 1905, so there was some connection with them. The Irish family, Ross Irish, could also be connected to Lavina and Laura through Lavina's third husband, Solomon Pettibone. Finally, a section to the west there was John Eastlick (44), his wife, Mary [Margaret](40), sons, John (19), William (17), Henry (14), Merton (10), and daughter, Cora (7). (See Plate 21 for the Eastlick geneology.)

They all farmed. John (he dropped the diminutive) was a farmer and a stock raiser. He was also known as a Republican and a member of the Methodist Episcopal church.[186] Alexander McDonnell, after he sold his land to his son, Angus, was renting. They may also have done lumbering. There is a photo from that period that shows a group assembling logs on the Mississippi (See Fig. 18). This may be the McDonnell family. So, in 1905, just a mile east of Monticello, near the Mississippi River there were some 25 people in this extended family (McDonnells, Freemans, Eastlicks, Irish) living neighborly together;[187] there must have been some interesting family potlucks.

The togetherness didn't last long. In that same year, March 1905, the McDonnells left the states and moved to east central Alberta, purchasing land near the town of Lougheed. The McDonnells still showed up on the 1905 Minnesota census because they made a return trip, sometime near the census date, June 28th, to settle up some things, but by fall they all had arrived in Alberta.[188]

In the late 19th century emigration to Alberta increased, both from the U.S. and from European coun-

---

[186]   Curtiss-Wedge, Franklyn. *The History of Wright County Minnesota, Vol 1*. Chicago: H. C. Cooper, Jr. & Co., p. 506.

[187]   There may even have been more; another neighbor in 1900 was the Charles Sutherland family; Manton Freeman, Lucy's brother, married a sister of Charles.

[188]   Lougheed Women's Institute, 1972, p. 248

tries. Cheap land was disappearing in the U.S., and Canada, particularly the southern parts of Saskatchewan and Alberta had land and climate similar to the great plains of the U.S. A large group of Mormons came to southern Alberta in the 1890s. They were followed by German Russians, Scandanavians (from Minnesota and the Dakotas), and Ukranians. In 1905 Alberta became a province and emigration increased as the land was surveyed and railroads brought the new province together. A land boom came to central and southern Alberta. The population of Alberta jumped five-fold between 1901 and 1911.[189] The western provinces of Canada were actively seeking persons from the states to emigrate to Saskatchewan and Alberta. An article in the *Wright County Times* (May 16, 1901) describes the climate as "all that could be desired" and the "prospects are of the brightest…the land is admirably adapted for stock-raising and dairy farming, as well as growing grain….the days of summer are full of sunshine, … autumn is characterized by an almost unbroken succession of fine weather, … winter is cold but extremely exhilarating and pleasant."[190] The land regulations in Alberta said that any person who is the sole head of a family or a male over 18 years old may homestead a quarter-section of available land. Generally, the person claiming the land had to appear in person at the land office, but someone else, a father or brother (as in the case of Angus), could register a claim by proxy. A person seeking title to the homestead had to be on the land, or within nine miles of the land, at

Fig. 20: Angus, Laura, and Donald
The child in front of Laura could be either Donald or Edna, depending on the date of the photograph, c. 1900-1904.

least six months of the year and cultivate the land for three consecutive years. A homesteader could also preempt a quarter section alongside his homestead for $3.00 an acre. This all must have seemed irresistible for the Freemans and McDonnells; land like this was no longer available in Minnesota.

Angus arrived in Alberta on March 17, 1905 (or in 1904) to check out the land and to file on six homesteads, for himself as well as the others in his extended family. The homestead he claimed was on section 36 (Twnshp 43, R.11) two miles east and north of Lougheed. He returned to Monticello to finish selling his land (and be counted in the Minnesota census). In the spring of 1905 he returned

---

[189]   MacGregor, James. 1981. *A History of Alberta.* Edmonton, Alberta: Hurtig.

[190]   A further inducement was tried by the Canadian Pacific Railroad. The railroad offered "Ready-Made Farms" on their land grants. These farms consisted of 160 to 320 acres. On each farm was a house, a barn, eight horses, five tons of hay, a well and pump. Fifty acres would be planted by the railroad with wheat, oats and potatoes. The land would be fenced and the houses painted and furnished. A settler could buy the Ready-Made Farm for 10% in cash (average $2000) and the remainder in nine yearly installments. Each community, such as Lougheed, was encouraged to appoint a welcoming committee for the emigrants. Some of these homes can still be seen on farmsteads near Lougheed. (*Sedgewick Sentinel,* March 16, 1911)

Fig. 21: The McDonnell Family
From left to right: Donald, Laura, Angus, Edna. This picture is said to have been taken in Alberta. The McDonnells came to Alberta in 1905, so if the picture were dated 1906, Donald would be 7 and Edna 3.

to Alberta and built a sod house and barn and harvested feed for the cattle. In December 1905 he returned to Monticello and some months later he gathered his family, Laura, Donald, and Edna, and moved to Alberta in the spring of 1906.[191] Before they left, on April 27, 1905, they sold some or all their land to Lavina, consisting of the SE ¼ of the NW ¼ of the NW ¼ (40 acres) of section 16, for $650.

Alexander, Angus' father, his wife, Lucy, his daughter Ella and son William came in October 1905. They homesteaded on sections 23 and 2 (Twshp 44, R11) just to the east and north of Lougheed. (See Plate 22.) Clark, Alexander's eldest son, remained in Monticello. Later this family moved to North Dakota and Clark died in Bismarck in 1958.

The Freemans also moved at this time. Sylvanus,[192] Manton, and Rupert, Lucy's brothers, LeRoy (Vance LeRoy), a nephew and his wife and two sons came from Minneapolis in 1906 and followed the others to Alberta. Lucy's mother, Caroline Freeman, remained in Monticello. Her husband, William, had died in 1885 and was buried in Monticello. She was 86 and the move probably was something she did not want to make. She died seven years later and was buried with her husband in Riverside Cemetery, Monticello.

In 1906, Aubrey McDonnell, Angus' younger brother, also moved to the Lougheed area (section 14, Twnshp 43, R11) with his family and farmed a homestead claim. Finally, a George Platt, described as a "confirmed bachelor"[193] and friend of the McDonnells also left Monticello and farmed a homestead claim near Hardisty, Alberta.

---

[191] The stories in the Lougheed history of the Freemans and McDonnells differ as to the year of their arrival; this may have resulted because several families moved during these years and there was travel between Monticello and Alberta by family members. [Lougheed Women's Institute, 1972]

[192] Sylvanus (1849-1909) lived in Minneapolis from the early 1880s to 1905. He worked as a bookkeeper. He died in Sedgewick, Alberta, as a result of injuries received when he was thrown from a horse.

[193] Lougheed Women's Institute. 1972, op. cit. p. 224.

It must have been quite a migration; the Canadians went back home and the Eastlicks remained in Minnesota.

Lavina's last move

In 1910 Lavina was still on her fifty acres in Monticello. But there were no McDonalds, no Freemans (Caroline, now 90, was living in the village of Monticello), no Sutherlands near by, and no Irish family. She was 72 years old, she owned her farm without a mortgage and she described herself on the census as a farmer on a general farm and as an owner working on her own account. Her son John lived a section to the west. He was 48, Maggie was 44, and three of his children were still at home: Harry (19), Merton (15), and Cora (12). Merton and Cora were in school. John described himself as a general farmer. The 83 acre farm was in Maggie's name and had a mortgage. Harry and Merton worked for him, and perhaps for other farmers in the area. And Charles Sutherland lived next door. Charles is now alone—no wife or children in evidence. If this is figured correctly, he would have been the brother of the great aunt who was the mother of his step-sister's husband; not really close as relations go, but perhaps they were also friends.

On February 24, 1915 Lavina sold her land, all 50 acres, for $800. She then moved to Alberta to live with Laura and Angus. There comes a time when the desire for independence gives way to the practical and Laura and Angus, both very kind and helpful people, probably prevailed on her to come and live with them.[194] Lavina was 83 and grandson Donald was 18 and granddaughter Edna was 13; perhaps Edna was a ready listener to the stories that her grandmother could tell. (See Plate 23 for Lavina's travels.)

Fig. 22. Angus and Edna
c. 1908, on the back porch of their home

Angus built a house for his family to replace the sod house where they first lived when they arrived in 1905. There was a bedroom on the first floor, perhaps for Lavina who might have had difficulty navigating the stairs. The home of Angus and Laura still stands. The house is pleasant even empty as it is today.

Laura was a story-teller according to her family. She and Angus were active members of the Seventh Day Adventist church and Laura taught Sunday school classes in the Groveland School, a rural school about two miles from Laura's home. Laura and Angus were also well-known for their gardens, vegetables, fruit, and flowers.

It was about this time that Laura must have signed and notarized the affidavit attesting to the authenticity of Lavina's published account. It was not official; the form was boiler plate obtained from Lincoln, Nebraska, and signed by Laura attest-

---

[194] The story of the McDonnells in the Lougheed history indicates that Lavina had gone with Angus and his family in 1905, but that doesn't account for Lavina showing up in Monticello in the 1910 census. The 1916 Alberta Census indicates that Lavina arrived in Canada in 1915.

Fig. 23: The home in Alberta
Angus and Laura lived here in Lougheed and this was Lavina's last home.

ing to the truth of the booklet. The only official part was that the signature was notarized.

Donald, their son, attended the Seventh Day Adventist Collegiate Institute at Lacombe, which is currently called the Parkview Academy, a preparatory school for the Canadian University College in Lacombe, and still operated by the SDA church. In 1918 he married Grace Folck. A daughter, Marie, was born in 1919. Five months later, on February 20, 1920, Donald died, likely a victim of the 1918 flu pandemic that killed 50 million people worldwide. His obituary said he developed double pleurisy and double pneumonia.[195] The funeral was held in the home of Angus and Laura and Donald was buried in the Lougheed cemetery. One can almost picture Lavina, standing on that windy hillside, looking down at the grave of another of hers. She had stood at the grave of two of her sons at Shetek, she had stood at the grave of another son in Rochester, and now she stood at the grave of a grandson. Children and grandchildren are not to die before their parents or grandparents. And, again as with all the family graves that Lavina stood over, there was and is no marker to name that grave.

Grace remarried to Oliver Koons and lived in Ohio (her original home where she was born in December 1898) and had two more children. She died in Co-

---

[195]   *Sedgewick Sentinel,* 2/19/1920

Fig. 24: Lavina and the McDonnells
On left, Edna and Lavina; on right, Laura and Angus; center, wearing a hat,
could be Donald and his daughter Marie. c. 1919.

lumbus, Ohio in 1973. Marie, their daughter, married Oliver Winfred Cass in
1948. They had one son, Oliver Cass, Jr. Marie died in 1986.

After the funeral Lavina returned to the home of Angus and Laura. She sat
on the back porch, enjoyed the gardens, and perhaps stood quietly looking at the
slough. On May 29, 1923 the *Edmonton Journal* published an article on her 90th
birthday. The article reviewed her life, noting that she has six grandchildren, six
great-grandchildren, two great-great-grandchildren, and a nephew in Nebraska.
Frank, Lavina's son who was wounded but never found at Shetek, is described as
"never seen or heard of." The article said "she is still enjoying good health only
absenting herself four times from the dining table for over a year on account of a
slight cold. She enjoys good eyesight and assists with the household mending and
light sewing as well as other small chores. During the last war she busied herself
with knitting for the Red Cross."

She died there on October 9, 1923. Her death was reported in Monticello and
Mankato; there was no notice in the county paper for Lougheed, but an obituary
was published on October 24, 1923 in the *Western Canadian Tidings*, a newslet-
ter of the Western Canadian Union Conference of Seventh-Day Adventists. The

Fig. 25: Lavina Eastlick
Lavina is third from left, Taken around 1920, Lavina would be 80 years old.

Fig. 26: John Eastlick, Monticello

Fig. 27: Laura's grave

obituary also reprinted the article from the *Edmonton Journal*. W. A. Schebo officiated at the funeral and his words of comfort were based on John 14:1-4.[196]

Angus registered her death in Lougheed on October 15; he used the name Lavina Eastlick. She was assigned a plot in the Lougheed cemetery, lot 83, block A, the north plot. In that record her name is misspelled as Mrs. Eastlake. In that plot on the hillside, presumably, she was buried. The *Western Canadian Tidings* noted that "a goodly number of her friends followed her to her last resting place in Lougheed, Alberta." Angus and Laura were there, and if Edna was around, she might have been there. John may have come too, but it was a distance and he was 61. Again in that strange ironic pattern, no marker was placed, nor is there a marker today.

John, still living in Monticello, died on January 22, 1942 and is buried in Riverside Cemetery in Monticello, next to his wife. Laura died on March 26, 1947. Her death was also registered, but the plot for her burial is not indicated. In the cemetery a temporary aluminum marker indicates the general area where her grave is. There neither was nor is a permanent marker for Laura. After Laura's death, Angus left the farm and moved to Edmonton to live with his brother. There he died on December 10, 1957. He is presumably buried there.

And then there is Edna, the adopted daughter. She seems to exist only on a line in the census. The family history just says that she lived in Alberta and British Columbia. Stories told about her describe her as unlike Laura and Angus. She smoked and drank, and, rumor has it, she ran off with a Royal Canadian Mounted Policeman. If half of what is said about her is true, she would have made life difficult for Angus and Laura. She died in Bowden, Alberta, on March 18, 1966. She is buried in the Lougheed Cemetery. A fine stone monument marks her grave.

---

[196] Let not your heart be troubled: ye believe in God, believe also in me. In my Father's house are many mansions: if it were not so, I would have told you. I go to prepare a place for you. And if I go and prepare a place for you, I will come again, and receive you unto myself; that where I am, there ye may be also. And whither I go ye know, and the way ye know.

Fig. 28: Lougheed Cemetery
Lavina's unmarked grave is to the left.

Edna is buried with the name Edna Grace McDougall, 1903-1966, with the family name, McDonnell (See Fig 29). Again, there is no record or similar burial place with the McDougall name in the Lougheed cemetery, nor do the names of Edna or her husband appear in the census records for British Columbia or Alberta during that time frame. The obituary of Edna says little. Her name is given as Miss Edna Grace McDonnell, it notes that she was born in the United States, her age at death was 62, she died in the Calgary Holy Cross Hospital, and she was survived by a niece, Mrs. Marie Cass of New York. The niece would have been the daughter of Donald, her brother. There is no indication why her gravestone includes the name McDougall.

The stories stopped when the third generation died. Some stories are still out there, but they are repeats and second hand. Over time the details blend into each other because there is no longer someone to say, "That's not so." Only Lavina's book remains to tell her story of Shetek; Lavina would smile, she still is victorious.

Fig. 29: Edna's grave

Where all the women are strong

Lavina is part of a company of women, for whom the description of women in Lake Woebegon[197] fits well: Mary Schwandt, Snana, Julia Wright, Urania White, Janette DeCamp Sweet, Old Bets, Justina Krueger, Alomina Hurd, Abbie Gardner, Sophia Smith, Cecilia Campbell, Susan Frenier Brown, Wasu-na-wun, Mariah Koch, Mattie Williams, Sophia Ireland, Louisa Myers, Margaret Hayden, Eci-ti-win, Sarah Wakefield, Julia Magner, Laura Duley, and dozens more.

Some went into captivity, some saved others from death or captivity, some comforted and helped others in captivity, some died, some lived and escaped, some saw children and husband killed, some saw husbands run away, some saw husbands killed protecting them, some hid, some faced down those who would harm them and their families. After the war, some never spoke of what they saw and experienced, some wrote about what they saw and experienced, some went insane, some left the state and never returned, some came back, kneaded the bread, and cleaned the kitchen. Some were Euro-Americans, some were Dakota Indians.

None were saints. But they did what had to be done. That's how Lavina saw it.

-

Fig. 30: Lavina's unmarked grave

---

197   For readers who are not Minnesotan, Lake Woebegon is a fictional town created by Garrison Keillor in his long-running radio program, "The Prairie Home Companion."

APPENDIX A
DIVORCE PAPERS

The Divorce of Lavina Day Eastlick and Henry Watson Smith

District Court
Blue Earth County

Henry W. Smith
Against
Lavina Smith

James Savage sworn for plaintiff.

I know parties, lived near them; she left the plaintiff about first June 65, she went off to Southern part of the state and was absent about 9 weeks; she asked me if I would take her son to board. Came to my house just before she went away and said she did not know if she would live with Smith any more. I have heard her say probably half dozen times since that she would not live with him any more. To the court, she once said she could not live with a man who did not love her or her children.

Judge Wilcox

Have known parties since 62. She told me in May or June 65 that she was not going to live with plaintiff any longer, was going away and soon went away. Told me where she was going, was going to peddle books etc. Have talked with her since she came back, last June, I think. Said she couldn't live with defendant [sic] any longer, thought she would do better to live by herself.

Plaintiff sworn.

Wife left me last part of June 1865 and we have never lived together since.

State of Minnesota, County of Blue Earth, the District Court 6th District.

The state of Minnesota to Lavina Smith, defendant.

You are hereby summoned and required to answer the complaint of Henry W. Smith, plaintiff to give a copy of your answer … at Mankato within thirty days after the service of this ?. Enclosure of the day of service and if you fail to provide said complaint as hereby required the plaintiff will apply to the court for the action demanded in the complaint.

Date July 30, 1866 J. T. Kennedy, Attrys for Plaintiff
Mankato, Minn.

The complaint of Henry W. Smith plaintiff by Mort. Gourtellatte and J. F. Kennedy, his attorneys, shows to the court that on or about the 1st day of April 1865 at the town of Mankato in the County of Blue Earth and in this state, the plaintiff was married to the defendant Lavina Smith whose name previous to said marriage was Lavina Eastlick and that they lived and cohabited together as husband and wife until sometime in June 1865.

That this plaintiff is now and inhabitant and resident of this state and has been such resident for more than one year immediately preceding the time of the exhibiting or filing of this complaint, and the defendant is also an inhabitant of this state.

That this plaintiff was forty five years of age on the 11th day of September 1865, and that the defendant or the plaintiff is informed and believes is about thirty-three years of age, but the plaintiff cannot now state the age more particularly.

That although the plaintiff has always conducted himself towards this said defendant as a father and dutiful husband, the defendant, disregarding her duties as a wife has willfully deserted and has been willfully absent from the plaintiff for the time of one year next preceding the filing of this complaint.

That these parties cannot live in peace and happiness together and their welfare requires a separation for the reasons among others, that their disposition and temper are uncongenial and they are unable to agree upon the most common and ordinary matters and difficulties were continually arising while they cohabited together.

That there is no issue of the said marriage of the plaintiff and defendant, wherefore the plaintiff demands judgment that the bonds of matrimony between himself and defendant be dissolved.

Mort. Gourtellatte and J. A. Kennedy Attorneys for plaintiff county of Blue Earth.

Henry W. Smith being sworn says he is the plaintiff in this action, that he has heard read the above complaint and knows the content thereof, and the said complaint is true of his own knowledge except as to the matters which and there in stated to be on information or belief which defendant believe to b e true.

Subscribed and sworn to before me this 30th day of July 1866.

Z. Radderts, Clerk Dist Court.

In District Court, County of Blue Earth.

Henry W. Smith vs. Lavina Smith

Filed July 30, 1866

Personally served the written summons and complaint upon the within named Lavina Smith on the 30th day of July 1866 by handing to and leaving with her a copy of the original.

Date July 30th 1866
Fees
Service $1.00
Mileage 10 miles 1.50
Paid July 26th 1867, 2.50
M.G. Walbridge, Sheriff Blue Earth County

First,

Defendant for answer to plaintiffs complain herein admits the allegations contained in the 1st, 2nd and 3rd numbers or causes of action in said complain except as to the time of marriage mentioned in the said first cause of action which plaintiff alleges was in the last day of March 1865.

Second

Defendant further answers said complaint and especially the 4th cause of action defendant denies the allegation that the plaintiff has always conducted himself towards defendant as a faithful and dutiful husband, and denies that she disregarded her duties as a wife or that she willfully deserted plaintiff or was willfully absent from the plaintiff for the term of one year next preceding the filing of the complaint in their action and denies further that she ever willfully deserted the plaintiff for any time what is as alleged
ʼ said complaint, but on the contrary defendant alleges that that the time of their said marriage plain-
⸍ owned and occupied a valuable farm of one hundred and sixty acres of land in the town of Mankato,

98

county and state aforesaid, and from which farm plaintiff and defendant immediately removed and there continued to live and cohabit as husband and wife until about the last of June 1866 when defendant was temporarily absent for a period of time not exceeding ten weeks upon business mutually beneficial to both parties and which business plaintiff had ? and agreed with defendant she should pursue and while defendant was so absent, plaintiff voluntarily and willfully and without any just cause or good reason deserted their home from said farm, and deserted defendant and willfully absented himself from defendant and their said home aforesaid, and did somewhere about the month of August 1865 leave the state of Minnesota and remain without the state of Minnesota and away from their said home until about the month of May 1866, when he returned to said town of Mankato, but refused and neglected to return to or live in his home aforesaid and did during all such time about August 1865 refuse and neglect to provide or furnish clothing food or sustenance of any kind whatsoever for defendant although defendant during all of such time lived upon said farm and took care of the same, and not withstanding the said plaintiff is worth at least the sum of two thousand five hundred dollars and as defendant only believes is really worth over the sum of three thousand dollars.

And defendant alleges that plaintiff will knew when he abandoned and left said farm and home in August 1865 that defendant intended to return to said home, and live and cohabit with plaintiff as her lawful and dutiful wife, but plaintiff willfully disregarding her duty and allegations to defendant as his wife deserted her as aforesaid with the express intent to prevent defendant from returning to said home and to prevent defendant from living or cohabiting with plaintiff as his wife. Defendant further answers said complaint says that during the said month of August 1865 she returned to their said home aforesaid in the town of Mankato where plaintiff and defendant had lived together as foresaid that she has two children by a former husband, both of them boys, one aged fifteen years and one aged five years, and that defendant together with her two boys aforesaid have been living upon said premises ever since the said month of August 1865 and have worked and occupied the same and cultivated crops thereon for their support and defendant has supported herself since the said plaintiff abandoned and willfully left defendant and their said home in August 1865.

Third

Defendant further answers said complaint and the fifth cause of action there in says that plaintiff and defendant can live in peace and happiness together as husband and wife if plaintiff will conduct himself in a proper and becoming manner and use language toward defendant in accordance with common decency as a husband ought to do, and defendant denies any and all allegations in said complaint to the contrary.

Defendant submits that plaintiff and defendant tempers and deposition are somewhat uncongenial but that this arises from the feverishness and ill nature of plaintiff, and defendant denies that the incompatibility or uncongeniality of temper is of such a nature or of such a degree so as to entitle plaintiff to a divorce, but that if plaintiff will control his temper properly he can live in peace and happiness with defendant.

Therefore defendant prays that said action may be dismissed with costs against plaintiff or as alternate relief in case a divorce should be granted by this court that defendant have awarded and adjudged to her by this Honorable Court the full proportion and amount of property of plaintiffs allowed by law in case of divorce and for such other and further relief as to the court shall seem just and proper.

Buck Freeman, Defendant attorney Mankato Minnesota August 4, 1866.

Lavina Smith being duly sworn said that she has heard read the foregoing answer and knows the contents thereof and that the same is true of her own knowledge except as to matters which are therein except as to the matters which and there in stated to be on information or belief which she believes to be true.

In district court, 6th district
State of Minnesota
County of Blue Earth
Henry W. Smith vs. Lavina Smith

The plaintiff in the reply to the answer of the defendant herein denies that he was consented that the defendant should leave home to perform the business referred to in her statement, but on the contrary he says he at all times opposed and objected to her going. He denies that the business the defendant left home to perform to wit the selling of books or pamphlets was in anywise beneficial to him. He denies that he ever consented she should leave home on such or any business but a few days at a time. He says she left during hoeing and just before haying commenced which aws the most inconvenient period of the year to the plaintiff. He also says she has conceived the idea of deserting him before she so left but concealed such intention from him. He says he remained at his home after the defendant left and performed the cooking and house work for a period of six or eight weeks whereby he became tired of living in that manner and went to visit his friends in the state of Connecticut. He utterly denies that he ever deserted the defendant or that he willfully absented himself from her. He says he did not leave until after the defendant had deserted him and further when he left solely for that reason and also for the reason that he got tired of living alone and doing his own house work.

The plaintiff also denies that he is worth either of the amounts alleged in said response and says he is worth not to exceed the sum of eighteen hundred dollars. He says he is informed to believe that the defendant is worth the sum of fifteen hundred dollars. Also that she has had and still has on hand a large amount of books or pamphlets from which she has frequently received and may receive considerable saving. He says she never has requested him to provide her any clothing food or sustenance since she left his home. He denies that he ever heard or believed that the defendant intended to return to live with him and he denies that he left his home to prevent her return there to or to prevent her living with him.

He denies that he ever conducted himself in any improper or unbecoming manner towards her on that he ever said indecent language to or of her. He denies that he has been peevish or ill-natured towards the defendant or that he had every given her any cause for deserting him.

State of Minnesota County of Blue Earth
In District Court, 6th District
Henry W. Smith vs. Lavina Smith

At a general term held at the court house in Mankato convening on the first Tuesday of December 1866.

This action having been brought to be heard after the pleadings in this action then having no appearance on the part of the defendant in the trial thereof testimony having been introduced on the part of the plaintiff from which it appears that all the material fact, charges in the said complaint are true, and that the defendant has been guilty of the several acts therein charged; on motion of H. W. Wait attorney for the plaintiff it is ordered and adjudged, that the marriage between the said Henry W. Smith plaintiff and the said Lavina Smith defendant be dissolved and the same is hereby dissolved accordingly and that the said parties are and each of them is freed from the obligations thereof and it is further ordered and adjudged that it shall be lawful for either of the said parties to marry again in the same manner as though said parties had never been married. Dated January 24th 1867.

Horace Hustin, Judge.

Entered this 24th day of January 1867.

APPENDIX B
FIRST PRINTING OF THE ACCOUNT

The First Printing of Lavina Eastlick's Account

From the *Grant County Herald*, December 2, 1862 p.2 c.1 & 2.

DAKOTA WAR, August 20, 1862 NEW ULM, MN
Indian Boundaries in Minnesota!
Murder of Mr. John Eastlick and his two children! perilous escape of the wife and 3 children.

It was remembered by most readers that among the numerous casualties of the Indians and the murder of whites in Minnesota, the murder of Mr. John Eastlick and two of his children and the perilous escape of his wife and her three surviving children were given in full detail shortly after, in the public prints. Mrs. Eastlick, bereaved wife and mother, with her baby past through Lancaster on Thursday last on their way to visit friends in this county, stopping overnight at the Mission House. Her brother, Mr. Leicaster Day, resides near Ellenboro and her brother in law, Mr. Sherman Cooley not far from Platteville. We called on the lady and asked her to relate the scenes through which herself and her family past, and which resulted thus sorrowfully. She assented and then related substantially what we write, we remarking that we designed the same as a narrative for publication.

The family removed from Ohio to Minnesota some four years ago, and settled in Olmstead County; thence about a year ago to Murray County, where they settled upon lands owned by them. They erected a cabin and improved a small field as a beginning. Eleven other families were settled in the same neighborhood. Mr. and Mrs. Eastlick had five children, all boys. We introduced their names and ages for convenience in our relation of details: Merton 11 years old past, Frank nine, Giles nearly eight, Fredrick five and John now one year old past.

Of a probable Indian attack of the 20th of August last, the settlers were warned about two hours before, when they immediately gathered to the house of a Mr. Wright. His house was deemed the best for defense as well as the largest for accommodating so many. Some preparations were made by the men who were all armed chiefly with shotguns, and they had plenty of ammunition. There were eight men in all, capable of making a defense. The Indians came up suddenly in a quiet and orderly manner, and sent word by one of their number named Pond, well known to the settlers pretending to be friendly that if the intended victims of their cruelty would come out from the house they should not be harmed. At last the settlers made up their minds to leave the house and then pick up things in wagons and leave for the present. The Indians appeared to leave them for the time without intention to molest them. But about a mile and a half on their way, the Indians came up, sixteen in number besides a reserve of squaws, all showing signs of anger but not yelling or uttering the savage war whoop. Supposing now that the Indians were but coming up to demand their teams, preparations were made to surrender these, with the wagons, in fact all, only so fast only what was dearest should be allowed to pass unharmed. The Indians took possession of the property, each mounting a horse, then commencing to fire upon the settlers. Our men then ordered the women forward for refuge in a neighboring slough, and then prepared to resist the Indians. Two of them ran away at the first fire and were not afterwards seen, leaving but six for defense. One of those who left had a wife to protect, and she was afterwards murdered by the Indians.

Mrs. Eastlick says he was about the last one she suspected of being a coward. The six now turned in and fought bravely successfully knotting or holding the Indians in check for a good while. But finally, the Indians appeared too strong, when our men fled for the slough afore said. The Indians followed and soon killed and captured nearly all. Mr. Eastlick was killed and the remaining five men were all wounded but succeeded in making good their escape and are now living. Three of the women and seven children were killed, and three women and nine children were taken prisoner.

APPENDIX C

Timelines of the Refugees

	August 20, Wed	August 21, Thur
Other	Smith reaches Plum creek (Burns brothers) at 3:00 p.m.. Warns the Bruns' brothers and they all leave Walnut Grove for Lamberton, reach Lamberton in evening?	Smith and the burns—Smith goes on to the Brown cabin. Burns brothers follow the Little Cottonwood, stay overnight on the prairie
Rhodes/ Dutch Charlie	Arrives at DC afternoon, warns DC and family; they leave; travel all night	Reach Brown cabin, house deserted, five miles beyond they find the bodies
Everett	Everett makes it to Dutch Charleys that night	Joins trail at Buffalo lake at night; gets near Dutch Charlies at night; sleeps overnight near DC
Duley	Leaves slough after battle, in evening	
Bently	Bentley gets to Dutch Charleys	Leaves Dutch Charlies, got to the Browns, all gone, found bodies, reaches Leavenworth in late afternoon. Town vacated; heard guns at Ridgely; refugees move into a vacant house; Myers and his son hide from some Indians when they are out foraging; Bently takes a quilt and moves into the woods because he fears that staying with the others would put him in danger.
Myer	Left Shetek in morning; went northeast and came on road 12 miles from his house; reached DS at 10:00 p.m., Bently and Everett comes at night	
Hatch	Leaves slough with Everett, travels at night, reaches DC, that night or next morning. Myers is there	
Merton Johnnie	Stay in slough over night	Leave slough, reaches Buffalo lake, stays overnight
Ireland	Stays in Slough	Leaves slough with Merton andJohnnie; falls behind the boys
Lavina Eastlick	7:00 a.m. Indians attack,, Slaughter Slough	9:00 am rain stops; 10:00 gun firing and children screaming;Finds dead in slough, wanders; 4:00 pm gun shots, children stop screaming
Hurd	Leaves Shetek, three miles from lake, 10:00 a.m. thunderstorm, sleeps on prairie that night	7:00 a.m., heard guns, near lake, found road 4 miles from lake, continued on road to dark

	August 22, Fri	August 23, Sat
Other	Burns brothers overtake Dutch Charley and family. They join with Dutch Charlie to get food. Burns hide in the4 woods, Mail carrier leaves Sioux Falls.	Burns start for Mankato, hide in woods overnight
Rhodes/ Dutch Charlie	Get to within 8 miles of New Ulm; Zierke and Rhodes? leave to find food; Indians capture t the others; Indians see scouting party, leave the Zierkes; they retrace route back to a cabin; Charley goes to New Ulm	In cabin; Mr. Zierke gets to NU and fights in the battle
Duley	8:00 a.m. goes into DC, leaves shortly, at 4:00 p.m. gets near the Cottonwood river, camps with Indians near Browns	Goes to the Brown house, finds the bodies. Goes to Lute Shitinger at 4:00 p.m., stays overnight
Everett		Group camps waiting for Mr. Myers to return
Bently	Traveled toward New Ulm along the Little Cottonwood, comes within 11 miles of New YUlm and sees smoke. At 11:00 a.m. sees some Indians with the who have taken the Zierke family captive.	
Myer		Myer leaves family and wagon and runs into NU, found Wright there; fought in battle, crossed river.
Hatch		Group camps waiting for Mr. Myers to return
Merton Johnnie	Daybreak, continues, overtakes Mrs.. Hurd at 5:00 p.m., reaches DC at dark, conceals themselves in cornfield	Leaves with Mrs.. Hurd and her children
Ireland	Makes his way to DutchCharley's	At Charley's; joins Lavina and mail carrier
Lavina Eastlick	Back at Shetek, stays at Ireland's, at night travels on road	Reaches Buffalo lake at 11:00 a.m.; meets mailman; reaches Charley's at 4:00 p.m.; camps 8 miles from Charley's
Hurd	Early in morning, 12 miles from Charley's, arrived at sunset, empty, stayed night in cornfield	8:00 a.m. Started to Browns, stayed on prairie

	August 24, Sun	August 25, Mon
Other	Burns reaches Mankato	Mail carrier continues to New Ulm
Rhodes/ Dutch Charlie	In cabin	In cabin; Zierke evacuates with the other NU residents
Duley	Came upon Elijah Whiton, goes to within 6 miles of New Ulm in Milford, Whiton killed. Duley crosses Minn R around noon	Arrives in New Ulm in the morning, goes with the evacuation
Everett	Waiting for Myers to return	
Bently		Hitched oxen to wagon and started to Mankato; camped overnight at a lake; Some 40 miles from Mankato milked cow
Myer	Mr. Myers crossed Minnesota river around 10:00 a.m. in morning with Tuttle and Wright; start for St. Peter, arrive in St.Peter	At St. Peter?
Hatch	Waiting for Myers to return	Hitched oxen to wagon and started to Mankato; camped overnight at a lake; Some 40 miles from Mankato milked cow
Merton Johnnie	Travel across prairie, united with mother and Tommy Ireland, reaches the Brown house	At the Browns
Ireland	Reaches Brown's cabin; stayed in the plum thicket	At the Browns
Lavina Eastlick	DAybreak, starts out; 10:00 sees Mrs... Hurd and children about noon; catches with Merton & Johnny two miles from Browns; reach house at sunset	At Browns
Hurd	Two miles from Browns met with Eastlick, postman, Ireland, reached house at noon	At Browns

	August 26, Tues	August 27, Wed
Other	Mail carrier returns, arrives at the Brown cabin at night.	Mail carrier leaves for Sioux Falls
Rhodes/ Dutch Charlie	Attempt to get to NU but fail; return to cabin	In cabin Rhodes is in St. Peter?
Duley	In South Bend and Mankato	At St.Peter?
Everett	Got fresh team of oxen ; at 4:00 p.m., 12 miles from Mankato they saw mounted men; tried to hide; it was Dan'e cavalry.	Arrived in Mankato.
Bently		Arrived in Mankato.
Myer	United with daughter and Smith, Duley, Rhodes at St.Peter	? Mr. Myers reaches Mankato; Mrs.. Myer's dies
Hatch	Got fresh team of oxen ; at 4:00 p.m., 12 miles from Mankato they saw mounted men; tried to hide; it was Dan'e cavalry.	Arrived in Mankato.
Merton Johnnie	At the Browns	At the Browns
Ireland	At the Browns	At the Browns
Lavina Eastlick	At Browns	At Browns; mailman returns from New Ulm, leaves for Sioux Falls
Hurd	At Browns	At Browns

Other		August 28, Thur	August 29, Fri
Rhodes/ Dutch Charlie	In cabin		In cabin
Duley	St. Peter?		St. Peter?
Everett	Mankato		Mankato
Bently	Mankato		Mankato
Myer	Mankato		Mankato
Hatch	Mankato		Mankato
Merton Johnnie	At the Browns		At the Browns
Ireland	At the Browns		At the Browns
Lavina Eastlick	At Browns, stays in field		Returns to Browns cabin
Hurd	At Browns		At Browns

Other	August 30, Sat	August 31, Sun
Rhodes/ Dutch Charlie	Leave for Mankato	Arrive in Mankato; finds husband
Duley	St. Peter?	St.Peter?
Everett	Mankato?	Mankato?
Bently	Mankato?	Mankato?
Myer	Mankato	Mankato
Hatch	Mankato	Mankato
Merton Johnnie	At the Browns	At the Browns
Ireland	At the Browns	At the Browns
Lavina Eastlick	At Browns cabin	At Browns cabin
Hurd	At Browns	At Browns

Other	September 1, Mon	September 2, Tues
Rhodes/ Dutch Charlie	Mankato?	Mankato?
Duley	St. Peter?	St. Petrer?
Everett	Mankato?	Mankato?
Bently	Mankato?	Mankato?
Myer	Mankato?	Mankato?
Hatch	Mankato?	Mankato?
Merton Johnnie	At the Browns	At Browns
Ireland	Starts for New Ulm	Arrives in New Ulm around noon; rescue party starts out, arrives at Browns cabin at midnight
Lavina Eastlick	At Browns cabin	At Browns cabin
Hurd		At Browns

	September 3, Wed	September 4, Thur
Other	Wright and Cook arrive at NU, joins soldiers under Lieut Roberts, arrive at Browns in evening	Browns family found 5 miles on way
Rhodes/ Dutch Charlie	Mankato?	Mankato?
Duley	St. Peter?	St. Peter?
Everett	Mankato?	Mankato?
Bently	Mankato?	Mankato?
Myer	Mankato?	Mankato?
Hatch	Mankato	Mankato
Merton Johnnie	Leave for NU with soldiers; reach NU at noon	At New Ulm
Ireland	At New Ulm	At New Ulm
Lavina Eastlick	Leave for NU with soldiers; reach NU at noon	At New Ulm
Hurd	Leave for NU with soldiers; reach NU at noon	At New Ulm

	September 5, Friday
Other	
Rhodes/ Dutch Charlie	Mankato?
Duley	St. Peter?
Everett	Mankato?
Bently	Mankato?
Myer	Mankato?
Hatch	Mankato?
Merton Johnnie	Mankato
Ireland	At New Ulm; leavs for Mankato
Lavina Eastlick	Leaves for Mankato, arrives in evening
Hurd	Mankato?

END

APPENDIX D

Poetry by the survivors

Uncle Charlie Hatch

Clara Hatch Brossard

Our dear old Uncle Charlie
A noble man and true,
Who away back in the sixties
Wore the army blue,
Has answered the last roll-call
And joined the ranks on high;
One more loved one to leave us
In heaven one more tie.

He was our youngest uncle
And the last one we had left,
One by one they've gone before him
Of them all we're now bereft.
We all loved our Uncle Charlie,
Close to him our hearts were bound;
But the ties are rudely severed,
Leaving us the cruel wound.

His life was quite eventful,
Strange, but yet so true,
If you would like to hear it
I'll tell a part to you.
His father and his mother
Died when he was but a boy,
And his life for sometime after
For him held little joy.

He came to Minnesota,
Which was then away out west,
With his brother-in-law and sister,
The one that he loved best.
They settled out at Lake Chetek
Upon a prairie claim,
Where they hoped they would gain
    riches
And make themselves a name.

They started out to build a mill
He and his brother-in-law Everett.
Upon the shore of Lake Chetek
(The ruin stands there yet.)
But e'er it was completed
They were forced to fly,
And Almira, his sister-mother
Doomed an awful death to die.

She and her two youngest children

By the Indians were slain,
Who took their scalps and left their
    bones
To bleach upon the plain.
And took her little daughter Lilly
With them in captivity,
For months she lived among them
E'er she gained her liberty.

Uncle Charlies had that morning
Rode on horseback near and far.
To alarm the scattering settlers
That the Indians were at war.
And they soon were running wildly,
Fleeing quickly for their lives,
But of all those eighteen families
Only a few were left alive.

Uncle Charlie was four times wounded
And compelled for days to lie
Hidden in the tall slough grass
With the Indians near by.
Everett too, was badly wounded
And he too, lay in the slough,
With his wounds so sore and bleeding
Hiding from those hostile Sioux.

But they finally escaped them,
Everett for days to lie
In a hospital at Mankato
Where they thought he would surely die.
Uncle Charlie soon recovered
And, with the soldiers went back west,
To find the bones of those who were
    slain
And lay them all at rest.

And then, for three years after
He served in our countrys' wars,
Fighting the rebels in the south
Beneath the Stripes and Stars.
He was a brave young soldier
And served his country well,
But all he had to suffer
I could never, never tell.

But when the war was ended

In eighteen sixty-five,
He married our Aunt Hattie
(She is still alive.)
And then a few years after,
I believe in sixty-eight,
He came to Minnesota
Again, to try his fate.

This time he was more successful,
Fickle fortune was more kind,
And a nicer home than he had
Would be very hard to find.
He settled in Martin County,
Near Huntley, on a farm,
And there for more than thirty years
Lived safe and free from harm.

Here he raised his seven children,
Three girls and four boys,
Of course they had their sorrows
But they also had their joys.
They were good and earnest Christian
Beloved by all around,
And in the church at Huntley,
Ever working they were found.

But heart disease upon him
Had lain its cruel hand,
And we knew that Uncle Charlie
Must obey its stern command.
But, his last act ere he left us
For a better world and joys,
Was to go to North Dakota
And take a homestead for his boys.

And far off in North Dakota
In a claim shanty, he died,
With no one but his faithful wife
And two sons by his side.
They brought his body back again,
In the old home once more to lie
Surrounded by fiends and kindred
Who came to say good bye.

Farewell, dear Uncle Charlie,
Dear old soldier, good and true.
They laid you in your coffin
In your Grand Army suit of blue.
With the stars and stripes around you
Folded close across your breast.
In your peaceful grave your sleeping;
One more spirit gone to rest.

Minnehaha, Laughing Waters,
Cease thy laughing once for aye,
Savage bands are red with slaughter,
Of the innocent today.

Ill accords thy sporting humor,
With their last despairing wail;
While thou'rt dancing in the sunbeams.
Mangled corpses strew the vail.

Change thy notes, gay Minnehaha,
Let some sadder notes prevail;
Listen, while a maniac wandr'er,
Sighs to thee his mournful tale:

"Give me back my Lila's tresses,
Let me kiss them once again;
She who blessed me with caresses
Lies emburied on the plain.

"See yon smoke; that was my dwelling,
That is all I've left of home;
Hark! I hear their fiendish yelling,
As I homeless, childless roam.

"Have they killed my Hans and Otto?
Did they find them in the corn?
Go and tell that savage monster,
Not to kill my youngest born.

"Yonder is the new-bought reaper,
Standing mid the ripening grain;
E'en my cow asks why I leave her,
Wand'ring, unmilked o'er the plain.

"Soldiers, bury her, my Lilla,
Place me also neath the sod.
Long we've lived and wrought together,
Let me die with her—O God.

"Faithful Fido, you they've left me,
Can you tell me, Fido, why?
God at once has thus bereft me,
All I ask is here to die.

"Oh my daughter, Jenny, darling,
Worse than death is Jenny's fate."

..

Nelson, as the troops were leaving,
Turned and closed the garden gate.

[But the Laughing Minnehaha
Heeded not the mournful tale;
What cares Laughing Minnehaha,
For the corpses in the vale?]

Attributed to Lavina Eastlick. Published in the *Mankato Daily Review* on January 17, 1918. A Mr. E. McCollum read the poem and asserted that Lavina Eastlick was the author.
It was not, however, written by Lavina. In was written by a Captain R. H. Chittenden who served with the first Wisconsin Calvary in the Dakota War and was with McPhail on the march to Ft. Ridgely in August 1962. On the road they encountered a settler, Charles Nelson He told them that his house had been burned, his daughter, Jenny, raped, his wife, Lila, killed, and he and his two sons, Hans and Otto, had fled from the Dakota. Nelson went with the troops and they came to his burned home. Nelson gazed about wildly, and, closing the gate of the garden, asked: 'When will it be safe to return?'" He apparently had gone insane. Sometime later, Captain Chittenden, while sitting under the Minnehaha Falls, wrote the verse. Harriet McConkey, not surprisingly, picked it up and included it in her book. The final verse is not included in the original. (See Harriet Bishop McConkey. *Dakota War Whoop.* St. Paul: Mosse Press, 1864. Pp. 194-1950

BIBLIOGRAPHY

BIBLIOGRAPHY

Published material

Albright, Samuel (with a preface by judge Charles E. Flandrau). 1898. "The First Organized Government of Dakota." *Collections of the Minnesota Historical Society*, Vol VIII. St. Paul: The Society.

Anderson, Gary Clayton and Alan R. Woolworth. 1988. *Through Dakota Eyes: Narrative Accounts of the Minnesota Indian War of 1862*. St. Paul, MN: Minnesota Historical Society.

Armstrong, Moses K. 1901. *The Early Empire Builder of the Great West.*. St. Paul: Pioneer Press

Bailey, Dana R. 1899. *History of Minnehaha County, South Dakota*. Sioux Falls: Brown and Saenger.

Bakeman, Mary, compiler. (2001) *Index to Claimants for Depredations Following the Dakota War of 1862*. Roseville, MN: Park Genealogical Books.

_____. (2009) *Emergency Aid for the Suffers from the Dakota Conflict*, Vol 5 1862-1863. Roseville, MN: Park Genealogical Books.

Board of Commissioners, ed. 1891. *Minnesota in the Civil and Indian Wars 1861-1865*. Vol. 1, St. Paul, MN: Pioneer Press.

Boutin, Loren Dean. 2006. *Cut Nose Who Stands on a Cloud*. St. Cloud, MN: North Star Press.

Bryant, Charles and Edward Neill. 1882. *History of the Minnesota Valley including Explorers and Pioneers of Minnesota and History of the Sioux Massacre*. Minneapolis: North Star.

Bryant, Charles S. and Abel B. Murch. 2001. *Indian Massacre in Minnesota*. Cincinnati, OH: Rikey & Carroll, 1863. Repr., Scituate, MA: DSI Digital Reproduction (page references are to the reprint edition).

Curtiss-Wedge, Franklyn, Comp. 1915. *The History of Wright County Minnesota, Vol 1*. Chicago: H. C.Cooper, Jr. & Co.

Dahlin, Curtis A. 2007. *Dakota Uprising Victims*. Edina: Beavers Pond Press.

DeCamp, J. E. 1894. Sioux Outbreak of 1862: Mrs. J. E. DeCamp's Narrative of her Captivity. In *Collections of the Minnesota Historical Society Vol 6*, ed. The Society. St. Paul: Pioneer Press. Pp 354-380.

Eastlick, Lavina. 1863. *Thrilling Incidents of the Indian War of 1862*. Lancaster.WI: Herald Book and Job Office. Pagination are from the latest printing by Murray County.

Folwell, William Watts. 1956. *A History of Minnesota* Vol. I. St. Paul, MN: Minnesota Historical Society.

———. 1961. *A History of Minnesota*. Vol. II. St. Paul, MN: Minnesota Historical Society.

Forrest, Robert J. Mythical Cities of Southwestern Minnesota. *Minnesota History*. Vol. 14, #3, 1933. 243-262

Forrest, Robert and J. D. Weber, compilers. n.d. A History of Murray County from 1833 to 1950. Sections of an unpublished history. Shetek Documents, Murray County Historical Society, Slayton, MN.

Hubbard, Lucius F. and Return I. Holcombe. 1908. *Minnesota in Three Centuries, Vol 3*. Mankato, MN: Publishing Society of Minnesota.

Humphrey, John Amos. 1915. Boyhood Remembrances of Life Among the Dakotas and the Massacre of 1862. In *Collections of the Minnesota Historical Society Vol XV*, ed. The Society, 337-448. St. Paul, MN: The Society. Pp. 337-448.

Keyser, Clark. 1915. *Old Rail Fence Corners: The A.B.C.'s of Minnesota History*. Ed. Lucy Leavenworth Wilder Morris, Ed. Austin, MN: F. H. McCulloch.

Kingsbury, George W. 1915. *History of the Dakota Territory*, Vol. 1. Chicago: S.J. Clarke Publishing Co.

Kinsley, Maxine Schuurmans. 2010. *The Sioux City to Fort Randall Military Road 1856-1892*. Sioux Falls, SD: Pine Hill Press.

Lawrence, Elden. 2008. *Stories and Reflections from an Indian Perspective*. Sioux Falls, SD: Pine Hill Press.

Lougheed Women's Institute. 1972. *Verdant Valleys In and Around Lougheed*. Lougheed, Alberta: Lougheed Women's Institute.

Luehmann, Maxine Kayser. 1982. *The Sun and the Moon, A History of Murray County*. [Minnesota]: Murray County Board of Commissioners.

McClure, Nancy. 1894. The Story of Nancy McClure. In *Minnesota Historical Society Collection Vol VI*. St. Paul, MN: Minnesota Historical Society. Pp. 438-460.

McConkey, Harriet Bishop. 1864. *Dakota War Whoop*. St. Paul: Wm. J. Mosses Press.

MacGregor, James. 1981. *A History of Alberta*. Edmonton, Alberta: Hurtig.

Moore, Frank. 1866. *Women of War; Their Heroism and Self-sacrifice*. Hartford, Connecticut: S. S. Scranton.

Oehler, C. M. 1959, 1997. *The Great Sioux Uprising*. New York: Da Capo Press.

Rose, Arthur. 1912. *An Illustrated History of Lyon County Minnesota*. Marshall, MN: Northern History Publishing Co.

Satterlee, Marion P.. 1915. Narratives of the Sioux War. In *Collections of the Minnesota Historical Society, Vol XV*. St. Paul: The Society. Pp. 349-370.

_____. 1915. The Battle of Acton or Kelly's Bluff. In *Collections of the Minnesota Historical Society Vol XV*. St. Paul: The Society. Pp. 3550364.

———. 2001. *Outbreak and Massacre by the Dakota Indians in Minnesota in 1862*. Ed. Don Heinrich Tolzmann. Westminster, MD: Heritage Books.

Schwandt, Mary. 1894. The Story of Mary Schwandt. In *Collections of the Minnesota Historical Society* Vol 6, ed. The Society, 461-474. St. Paul, MN: Pioneer Press.

Silvernale, John A. 1970 (3rd printing). *In Commemoration of the Sioux Uprising August 20, 1862*. Slayton, MN: Murray County Historical Society.

Smith, Charles. 1949. *A Comprehensive History of Minnehaha County, South Dakota*. Mitchell, SD: Educator Supply Co.

Sneve, Virginia Driving Hawk. 1974. *Betrayed*. New York: Holiday House.

Wakefield, Sarah F. 1997. *Six Weeks in the Sioux Tepees: A Narrative of Indian Captivity*. Ed. June Namais. Norman, OK: University of Oklahoma Press.

White, N. D. 1901. Captivity Among the Sioux, August 19 to September 26, 1862. In *Collections of the Minnesota Historical Society, Vol. IX*, ed. Minnesota Historical Society, 404-434. St. Paul, MN: The Society. Pp. 395-426.

Wingerd, Mary Lethert. 2010. *North County: The Making of Minnesota*. Minneapolis: University of Minnesota Press.

Workman, Harper. 1924. Early History of Lake Shetek County. An unpublished typed manuscript. Shetek Collection, Brown County Museum, Brown County Historical Society, New Ulm, MN.

Index

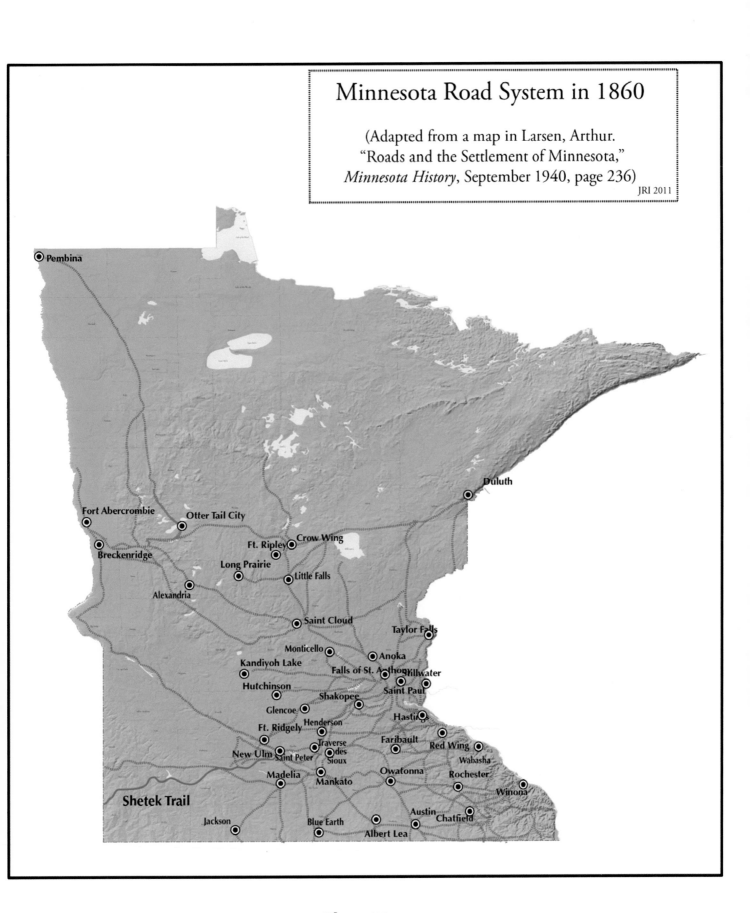

Minnesota Road System in 1860

(Adapted from a map in Larsen, Arthur.
"Roads and the Settlement of Minnesota,"
Minnesota History, September 1940, page 236)

JRI 2011

Plate #1

Selected Trails in Southern Minnesota 1860

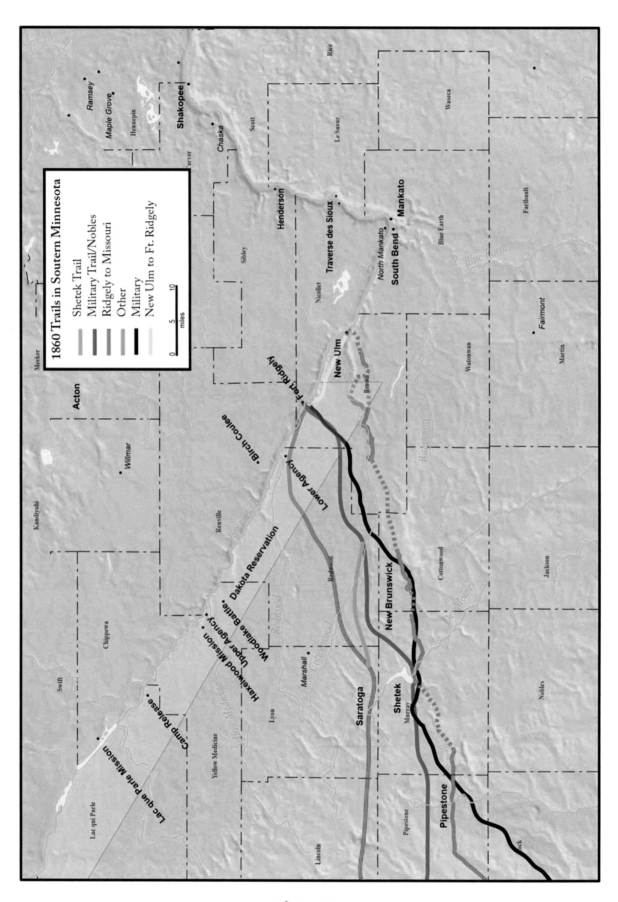

1860 Trails in Southern Minnesota

- Shetek Trail
- Military Trail/Nobles
- Ridgely to Missouri
- Other
- Military
- New Ulm to Ft. Ridgely

0 5 10
miles

Plate #2

The Bogus 1857 Census of Cornwall City, Murray County, Minnesota

CENSUS.---- Inhabitants of _Cornwall City_ in the County of _Murray_ ___ Territory of Minnesota, enumerated by me this _27_ day of _Oct_ A.D. 1857.

N R Brown Ass't Marshal.

		NAME of every person whose usual place of abode on the 31st day of September, 1857.	Age	Sex	Color	PLACE OF BIRTH.	VOTERS. Native	VOTERS. Naturalized	OCCUPATION, If any, of each male person over fifteen years of age.	
1	1	Parker K Anderson	55	m		North Carolina	1		Blacksmith	1
		Lewis Howe	24	m		Mass	1		Laborer	2
		Orson Rodgers	27	m		Ohio	1		Laborer	3
2	2	Wm S Lawrance	29	m		Vermont	1		Farmer	4
		Patrick Coalder	24	m		Ireland		0	Laborer	5
		James Northrup	31	m		Maine	1		Carpenter	6
3	3	Frederick Warndorff	35	m		Germany		0	Farmer	7
		Caroline Warndorff	28	f		Germany				8
		Frederick Warndorff	8	m		Ohio				9
		Martha Warndorff	5	f		Ohio				10
		John Warndorff	3	m		Ohio				11
		Mary Warndorff	½	f		Iowa				12
		Jacob Warndorff	19	m		Germany			Farmer	13
4	4	Robert Kickenhaus	56	m		Germany		0	Farmer	14
		Peter Saftus	26	m		Germany		0	Laborer	15
		Abraham Smith	24	m		Pennsylvania	1		Laborer	16
5	5	Wm S Sowren	44	m		New Jersey	1		Farmer	17
		Patience Sowren	39	f		Kentucky				18
		Towers Sowren	22	m		Ohio	1		Farmer	19
		Rebecka Sowren	19	f		Michigan				20
		Ruth Sowren	16	f		Michigan				21
		Luther Sowren	11	m		Michigan				22
		John W Sowren	8	m		Illinois				23
		Robert Sowren	6	m		Illinois				24
		Sarah Sowren	4	f		Illinois				25
		Timothy Sowren	1	m		Iowa				26
6	6	Robert Conway	29	m		New York	1		Farmer	27
		James Buckner	24	m		Vermont	1		Laborer	28
		James Conway	26	m		New York	1		Farmer	29
		Rigas Knop	27	m		Maine	1		Laborer	30
7	7	Charles W Lawrance	34	m		Vermont	1		Farmer	31
		Moses Moran	56	m		Upper Canada		0	Potter	32
		Cantwell Cobb	22	m		Maryland	1		Shoemaker	33
		Roger Knop	24	m		Maine	1		Teamster	34
8	8	Thomas Carter	38	m		Pennsylvania			Farmer	35
		Lydia Ann Carter	25	f		Ohio				36
		Lafayette Carter	5	m		Indiana				37
		Mary Ann Carter	2	f		Indiana				38
		Martha Jane Carter	½	f		Minnesota				39
		Horace Carter	18	m		Pennsylvania			Farmer	40

Plate #3

1860 Federal Census of Murray County

579

SCHEDULE 1.—Free Inhabitants in _____ in the County of _Murray_ State of _Minnesota_ enumerated by me, on the _2d_ day of _July_ 1860. _Po Pearson_ Ass't Marshal.

Post Office _Mankato & New Ulm._

		The name of every person whose usual place of abode on the first day of June, 1860, was in this family	Age	Sex	Color	Profession, Occupation, or Trade of each person, male and female, over 15 years of age	Value of Real Estate	Value of Personal Estate	Place of Birth, Naming the State, Territory, or Country.	Married within the year	Attended School within the year	Persons over 20 y'rs of age who cannot read & write	Whether deaf and dumb, blind, insane, idiotic, pauper, or convict.	
		3	4	5	6	7	8	9	10	11	12	13	14	
1	525 488	Henry W. Smith	40	M		Farmer		100	Mass.					1
2		Sophia "	30	F					Do					2
3	526 489	Aaron Myers	35	M					New York					3
4		Mary "	34	F					Do					4
5		Louisa "	11	F					Do		1			5
6		Arthur "	9	M					Do		1			6
7		Eliza "	6	F					Do		1			7
8		Frederick "	4	M					Wisconsin					8
9	527 490	Hoyle Pomeroy	25	M		Farmer		300	New York					9
10		William Barrett	30	M		do	500	100	New Jersey					10
11		Alvira "	27	F					Ohio					11
12		Lilian "	4	F					Wisconsin					12
13		Edward "	1	M					Do					13
14	528 491	John Wright	25	M		Farmer	500	75	Illinois					14
15		Julia "	23	F					Michigan					15
16		Aldora "	3	F					Wisconsin					16
17		George "	1	M					Minnesota					17
18		John M. Bee	35	M		Farmer		100	Indiana					18
19	529 492	Phineas B. Hard	27	M		do		500	New York					19
20		Almira "	24	F					Do					20
21		W. Henry "	1	M					Wisconsin					21
22		Christina "	70	F					New York					22
23	530 493	John Coch	34	M		Farmer		500	Wisconsin					23
24		Magina "	30	F					Saxony					24
25	531 494	George S. Lane	35	M		Farmer		300	Ohio					25
26		Laura "	32	F					New York					26
27		Francis "	10	F					Michigan		1			27
28		Emma "	4	F					Wisconsin					28
29		Alice "	2	F					Do					29
30														30
31					Concluded								31
32														32
33														33
34														34
35														35
36														36
37														37
38														38
39														39
40														40

No. white males 14   No. colored males ___   No. foreign born ___   No. blind ___   No. idiotic ___

No. white females 11   No. colored females ___   No. deaf and dumb ___   No. insane ___   1000   2875   No. pauper ___   No. convicts ___

27

Plate #4

1861 Survey Map
Murray Township
Murray County
with post road between New Ulm and Sioux Falls

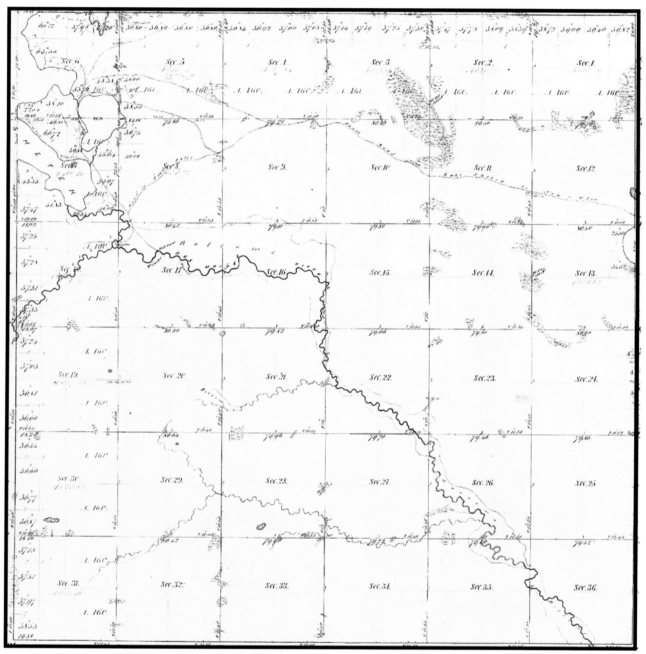

Plate #5

Johnson's Map of Minnesota 1865. Published by Johnson & Ward

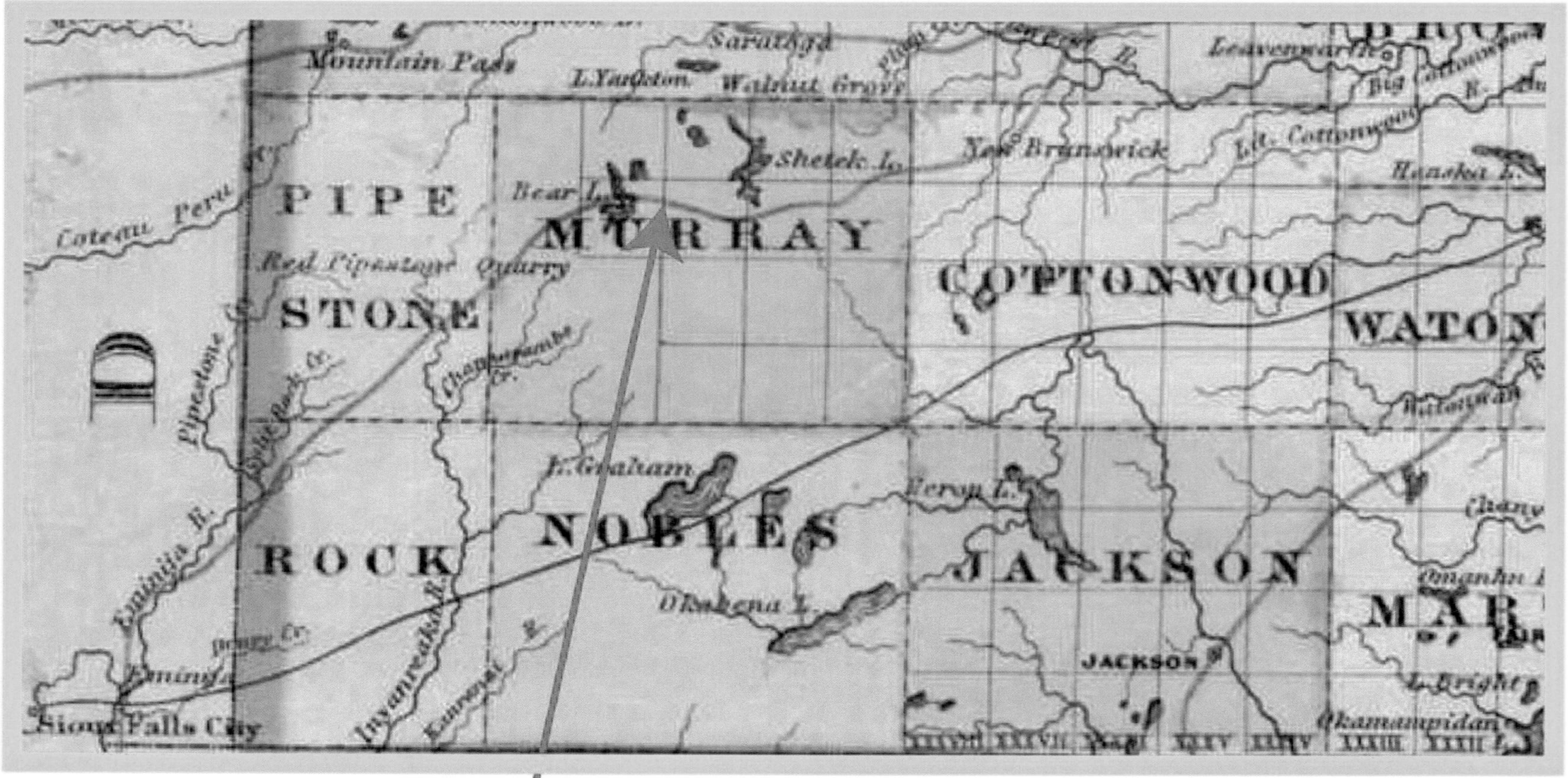

Southwest quarter of the Johnson Map showing a portion of the New Ulm to Sioux Falls mail route.

New Ulm to Sioux Falls route

Plate #6

The Shetek Trail in Eastern Brown County

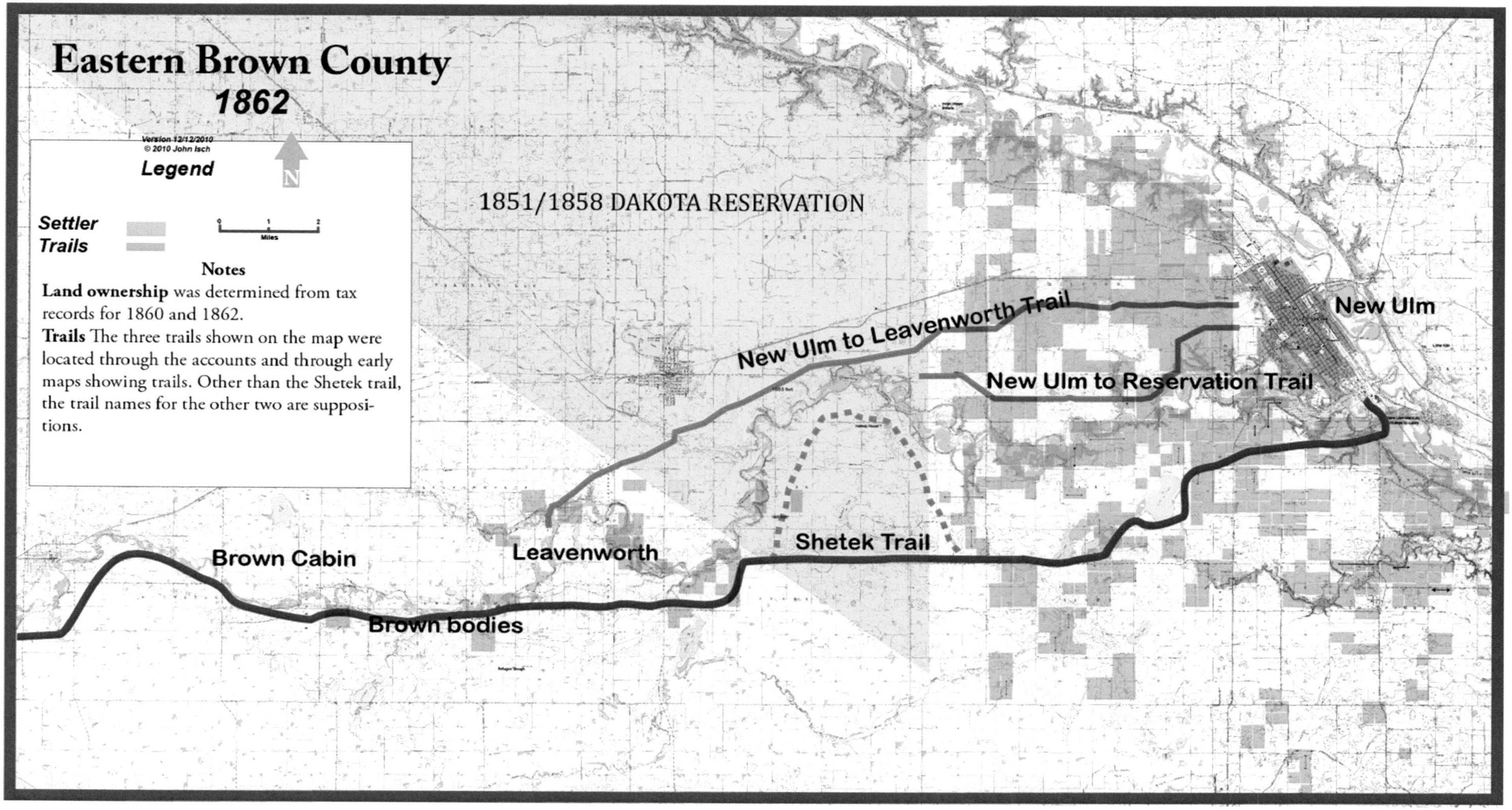

Eastern Brown County
1862

New Ulm

New Ulm to Reservation Trail

New Ulm to Leavenworth Trail

Shetek Trail

Leavenworth

Brown Cabin

Brown bodies

1851/1858 DAKOTA RESERVATION

Version 12/12/2010
© 2010 John Isch

Legend

Settler Trails

Trails

Notes

Land ownership was determined from tax records for 1860 and 1862.

Trails The three trails shown on the map were located through the accounts and through early maps showing trails. Other than the Shetek trail, the trail names for the other two are suppositions.

Miles
0   1   2

N

Plate #7

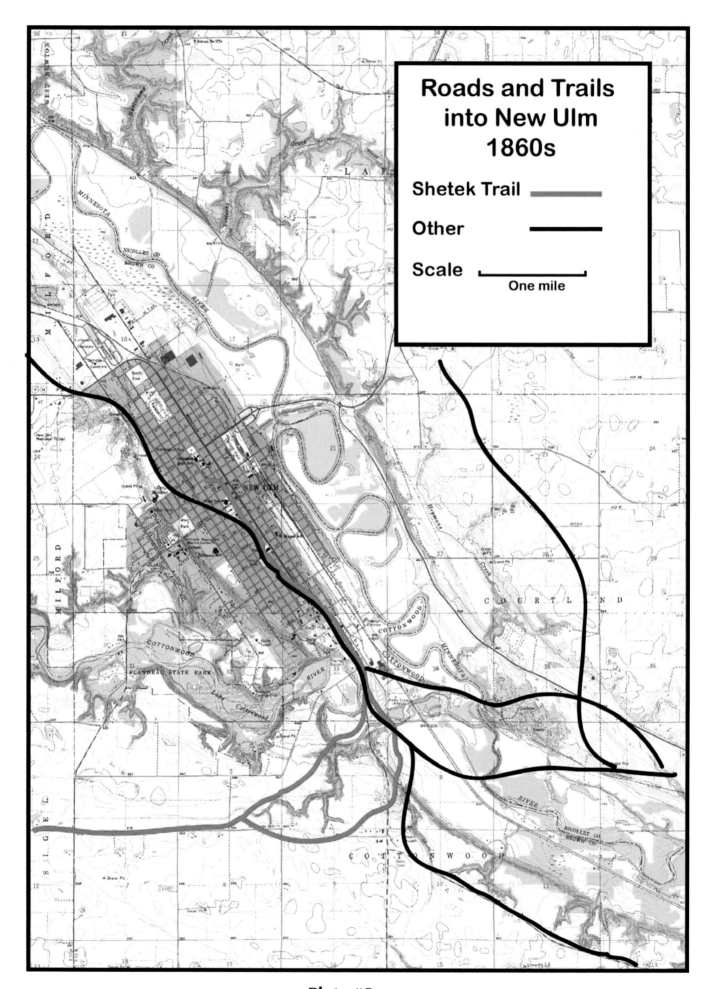

Roads and Trails
into New Ulm
1860s

Shetek Trail

Other

Scale

One mile

Plate #8

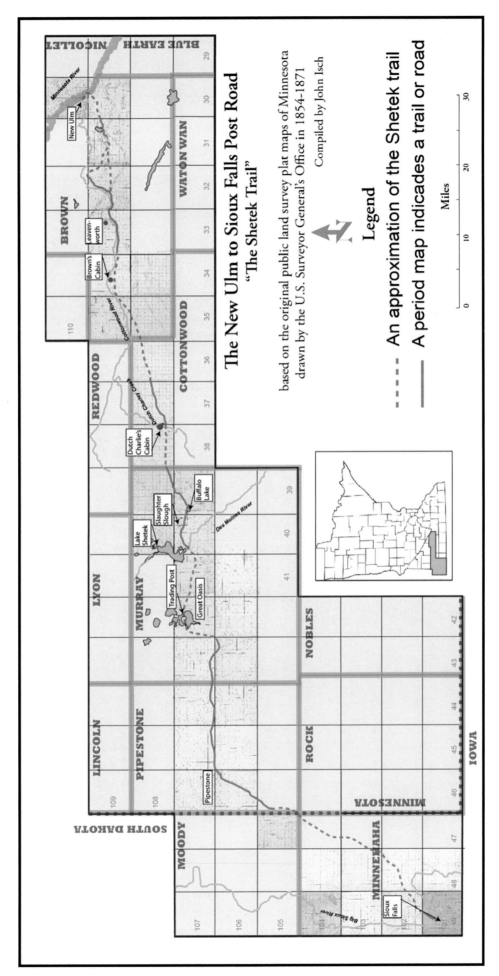

The New Ulm to Sioux Falls Post Road
"The Shetek Trail"

based on the original public land survey plat maps of Minnesota
drawn by the U.S. Surveyor General's Office in 1854-1871

Compiled by John Isch

Legend

- - - - An approximation of the Shetek trail

———— A period map indicades a trail or road

Plate #9

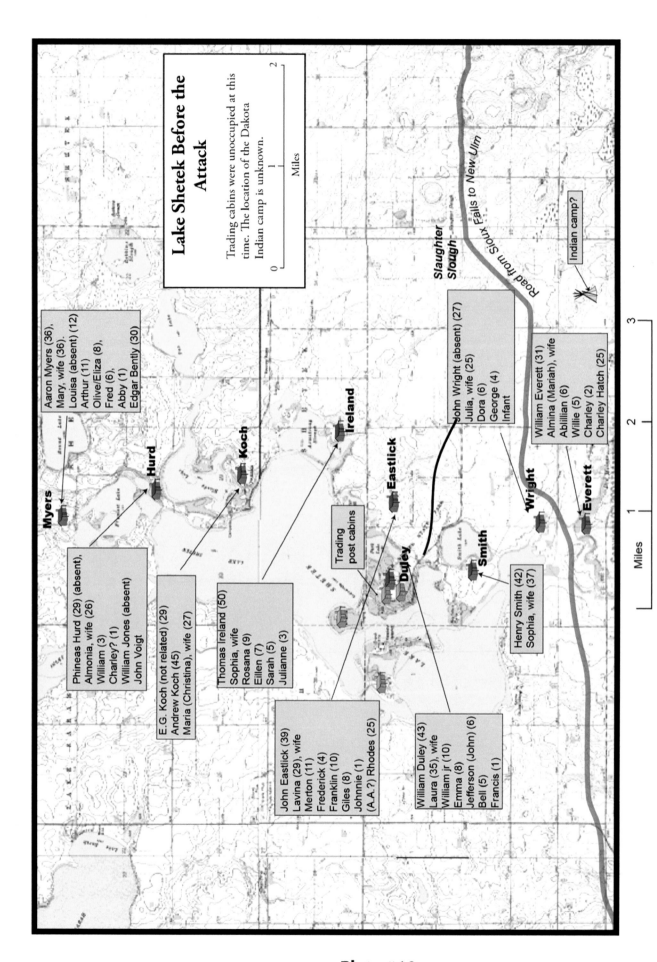

Lake Shetek Before the Attack

Trading cabins were unoccupied at this time. The location of the Dakota Indian camp is unknown.

Aaron Myers (36),
Mary, wife (36).
Louisa (absent) (12)
Arthur (11)
Olive/Eliza (8),
Fred (6),
Abby (1)
Edgar Bently (30)

Phineas Hurd (29) (absent),
Almonia, wife (26)
William (3)
Charley? (1)
William Jones (absent)
John Voigt

E.G. Koch (not related) (29)
Andrew Koch (45)
Maria (Christina), wife (27)

Thomas Ireland (50)
Sophia, wife
Rosana (9)
Eillen (7)
Sarah (5)
Julianne (3)

John Eastlick (39)
Lavina (29), wife
Merton (11)
Frederick (4)
Franklin (10)
Giles (8)
Johnnie (1)
(A.A.?) Rhodes (25)

William Duley (43)
Laura (35), wife
William jr (10)
Emma (8)
Jefferson (John) (6)
Bell (5)
Francis (1)

John Wright (absent) (27)
Julia, wife (25)
Dora (6)
George (4)
Infant

William Everett (31)
Almina (Mariah), wife
Ablillian (6)
Willie (5)
Charley (2)
Charley Hatch (25)

Henry Smith (42)
Sophia, wife (37)

Trading post cabins

Myers
Hurd
Koch
Ireland
Eastlick
Duley
Smith
Wright
Everett

Slaughter Slough

Road from Sioux Falls to New Ulm

Indian camp?

Miles
0   1   2

Miles
1   2   3

Plate #10

Shetek Timeline

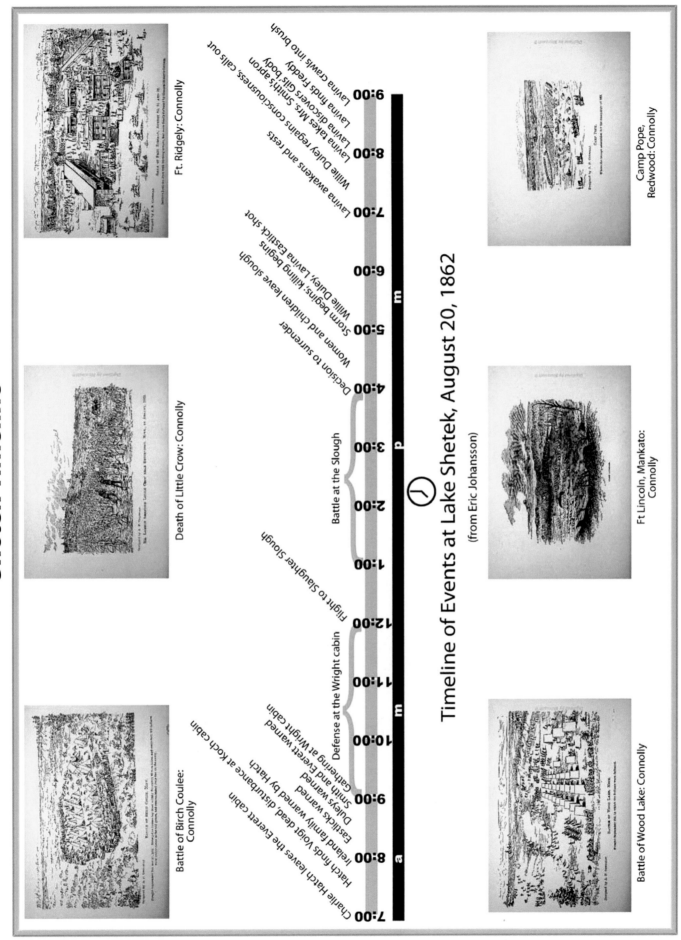

Ft. Ridgely: Connolly

Death of Little Crow: Connolly

Battle of Birch Coulee: Connolly

Camp Pope, Redwood: Connolly

Ft Lincoln, Mankato: Connolly

Battle of Wood Lake: Connolly

Timeline of Events at Lake Shetek, August 20, 1862

(from Eric Johansson)

Lavina crawls into brush
Lavina finds Freddy
Lavina discovers Gill's body
Lavina takes Mrs. Smith's apron
Willie Dudley regains consciousness, calls out
Lavina awakens and rests
Willie Dudley begins killing; Lavina Eastlick shot
Storm begins; killing begins
Women and children leave slough
Decision to surrender
Battle at the Slough
Flight to Slaughter Slough
Defense at the Wright cabin
Gathering at Wright cabin
Smith and Everett warned
Dudleys warned
Ireland family warned by Hatch
Eastlicks warned, disturbance at Koch cabin
Charlie Hatch leaves the Everett cabin
Hatch finds Voigt dead, disturbance at Koch cabin

6:00 8:00 7:00 6:00 5:00 4:00 3:00 2:00 1:00 12:00 11:00 10:00 9:00 8:00 7:00

Plate #11

Mrs. Hurd's Route to New Ulm

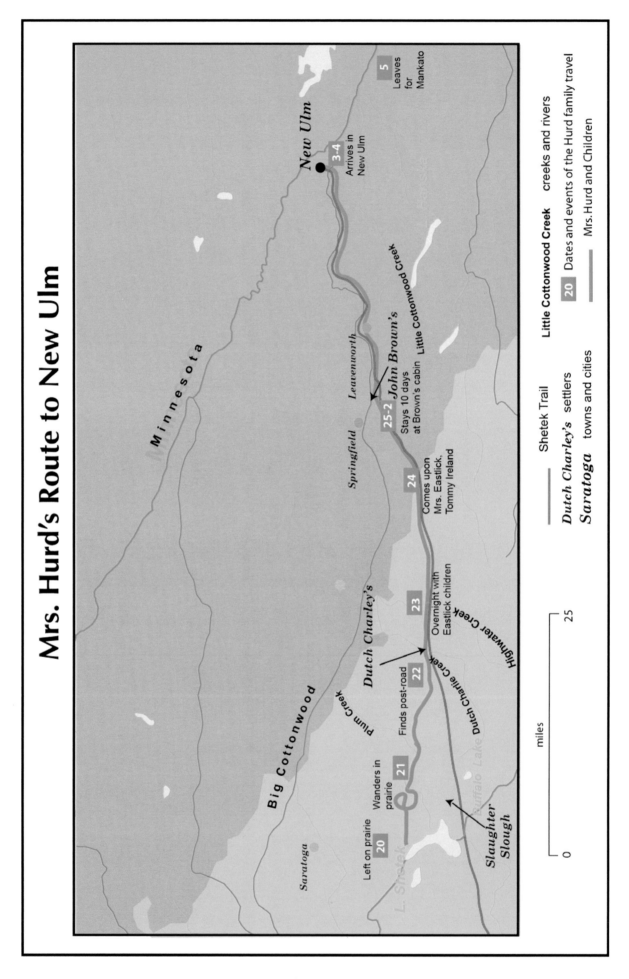

Plate #12

Lake Shetek Following the Attack

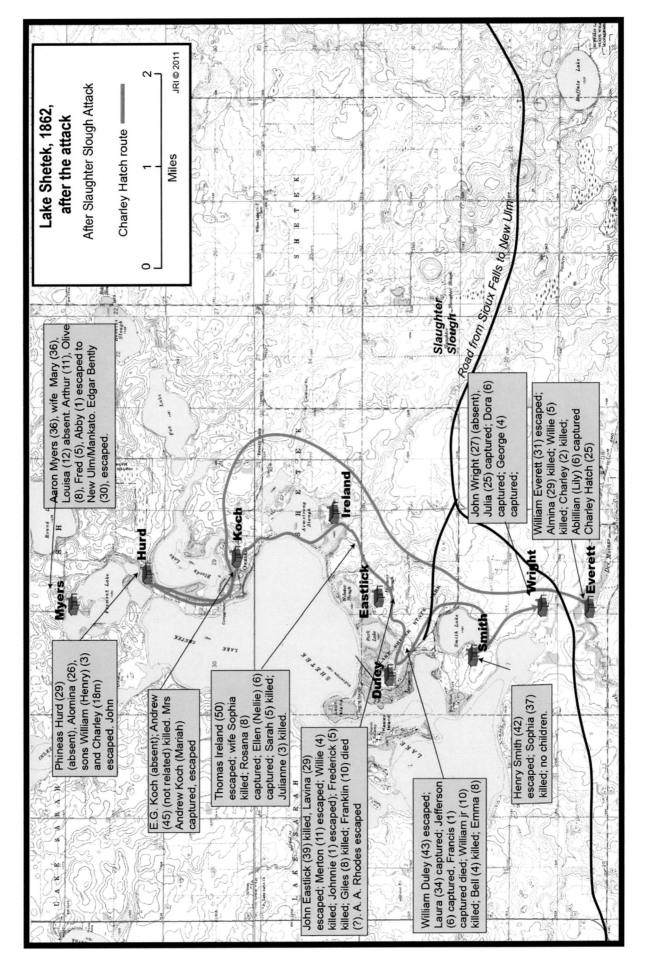

Lake Shetek, 1862, after the attack

After Slaughter Slough Attack

Charley Hatch route

Miles

0   1   2

JRI © 2011

Aaron Myers (36), wife Mary (36), Louisa (12) absent. Arthur (11), Olive (8), Fred (5), Abby (1) escaped to New Ulm/Mankato. Edgar Bently (30), escaped.

Phineas Hurd (29) (absent), Alomina (26), sons William (Henry) (3) and Charley (18m) escaped. John

E.G. Koch (absent); Andrew (45) (not related) killed. Mrs Andrew Koch (Mariah) captured, escaped

Thomas Ireland (50) escaped; wife Sophia killed; Rosana (8) captured; Ellen (Nellie) (6) captured; Sarah (5) killed; Julianne (3) killed.

John Eastlick (39) killed, Lavina (29) escaped; Merton (11) escaped; Willie (4) killed; Johnnie (1) escaped; Frederick (5) killed; Giles (8) killed; Franklin (10) died (?). A. A. Rhodes escaped

William Duley (43) escaped; Laura (34) captured; Jefferson (6) captured, Francis (1) captured died; William jr (10) killed; Bell (4) killed; Emma (8) killed.

Henry Smith (42) escaped; Sophia (37) killed; no children.

John Wright (27) (absent), Julia (25) captured; Dora (6) captured; George (4) captured;

William Everett (31) escaped; Almina (29) killed; Willie (5) killed; Charley (2) killed; Abillian (Lily) (6) captured Charley Hatch (25)

Road from Sioux Falls to New Ulm

Slaughter Slough

Myers

Hurd

Koch

Ireland

Eastlick

Duley

Smith

Wright

Everett

LAKE SHETEK

Plate #13

Scene 8: The Flight

John Stevens, Panorama of the Indian Massacre of 1862 and the Black Hills.

Gilcrease Museum, Tulsa OK

Plate #14

Scene 10: Slaughter Slough

John Stevens, Panorama of the Indian Massacre of 1862 and the Black Hills.

Gilcrease Museum, Tulsa OK

Plate #15

Scene 11: Merton & Johnnie Eastlick

Plate #16

Lavina Eastlick's Route to New Ulm

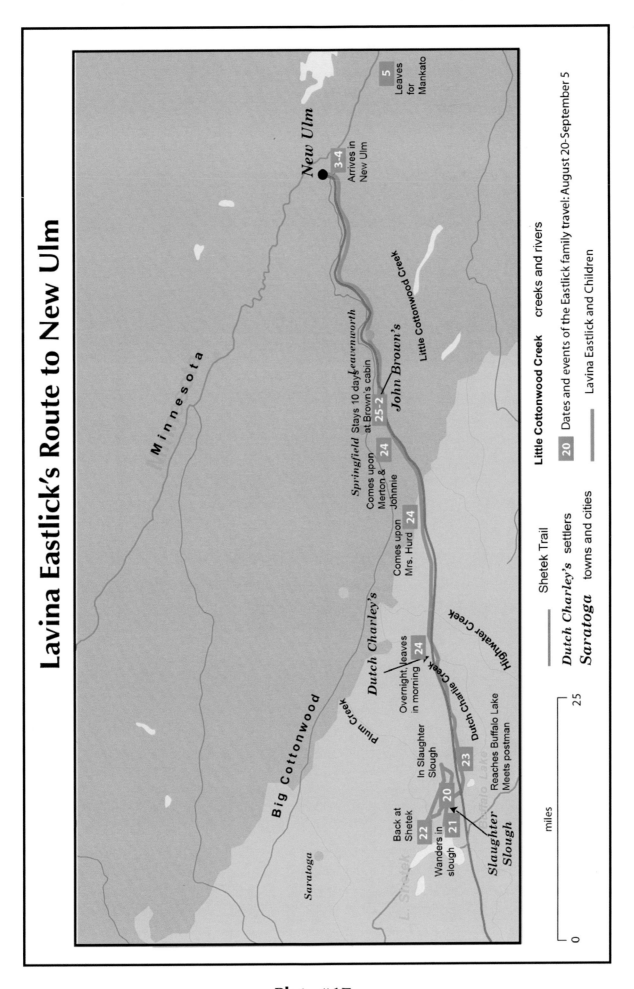

New Ulm

3-4 Arrives in New Ulm

5 Leaves for Mankato

Minnesota

Little Cottonwood Creek

John Brown's

Leavenworth

25-2 Stays 10 days at Brown's cabin

24 *Springfield* Comes upon Merton & Johnnie

24 Comes upon Mrs. Hurd

Big Cottonwood

Plum Creek

Dutch Charley's

24 Overnight, leaves in morning

Highwater Creek

23 Reaches Buffalo Lake Meets postman

Dutch Charlie Creek

20 In Slaughter Slough

22 Back at Shetek

21 Wanders in slough

Saratoga

Buffalo Lake

L. Shetek

Slaughter Slough

Little Cottonwood Creek creeks and rivers

20 Dates and events of the Eastlick family travel: August 20-September 5

Lavina Eastlick and Children

Shetek Trail

Dutch Charley's settlers

Saratoga towns and cities

miles

0   25

Plate #17

Mankato, Minnesota: Lavina Eastlick

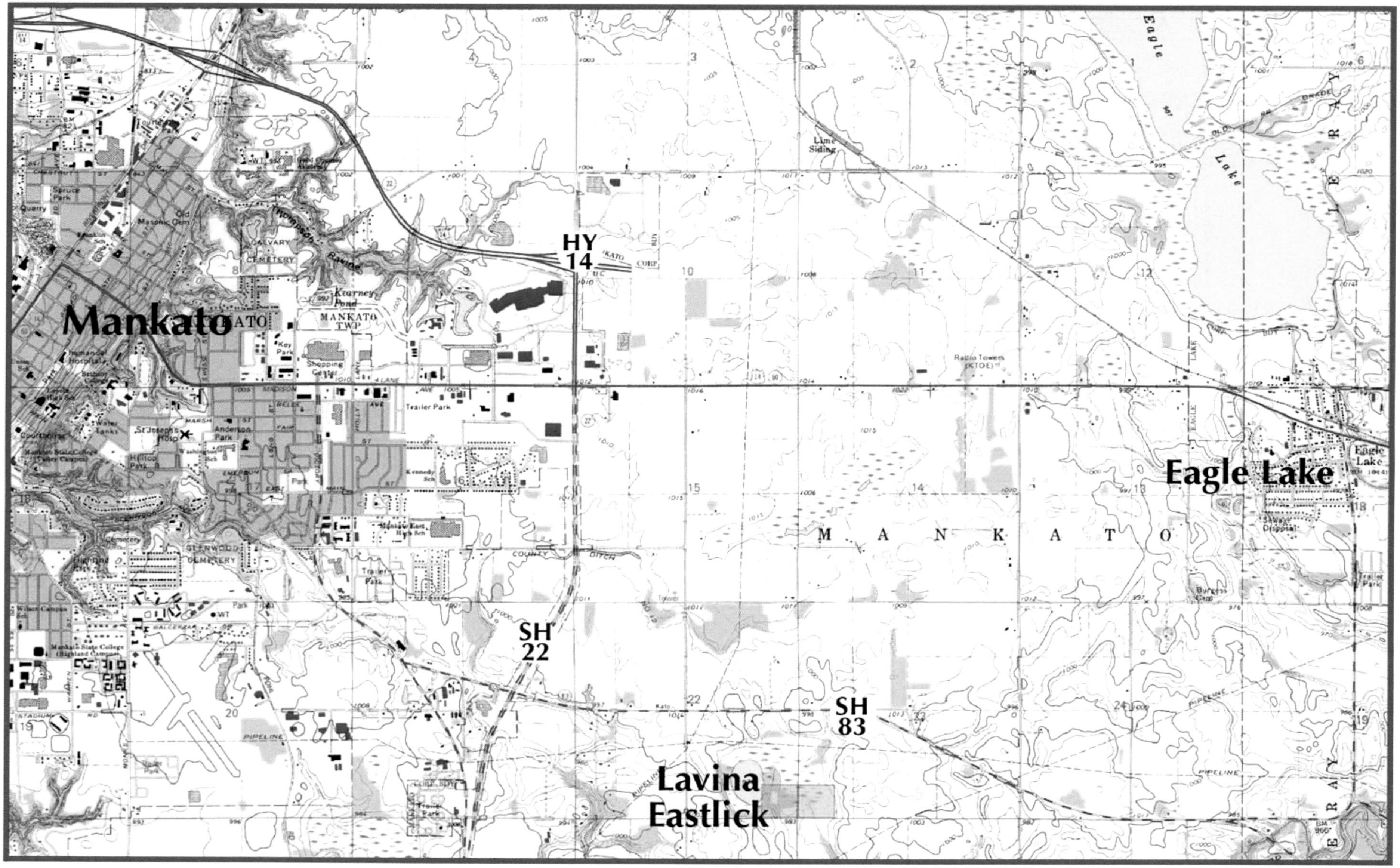

Eagle Lake

Lavina Eastlick

SH 83

SH 22

HY 14

Mankato

Plate #18

Monticello, Minnesota: Freemans, McDonnells, Eastlicks

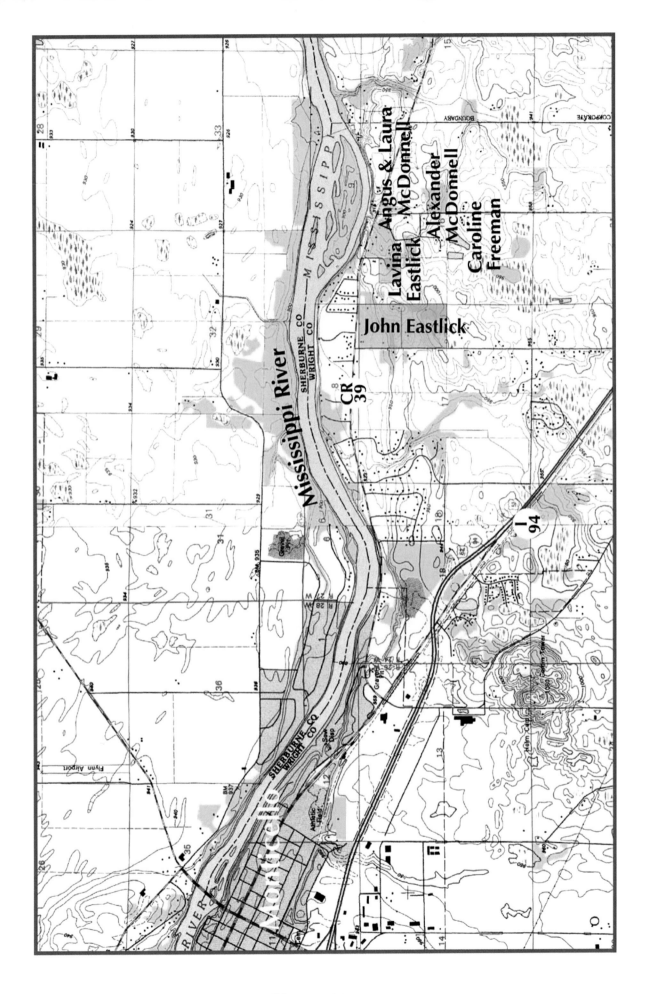

Plate #19

Wright County, Monticello Minnesota Census 1905

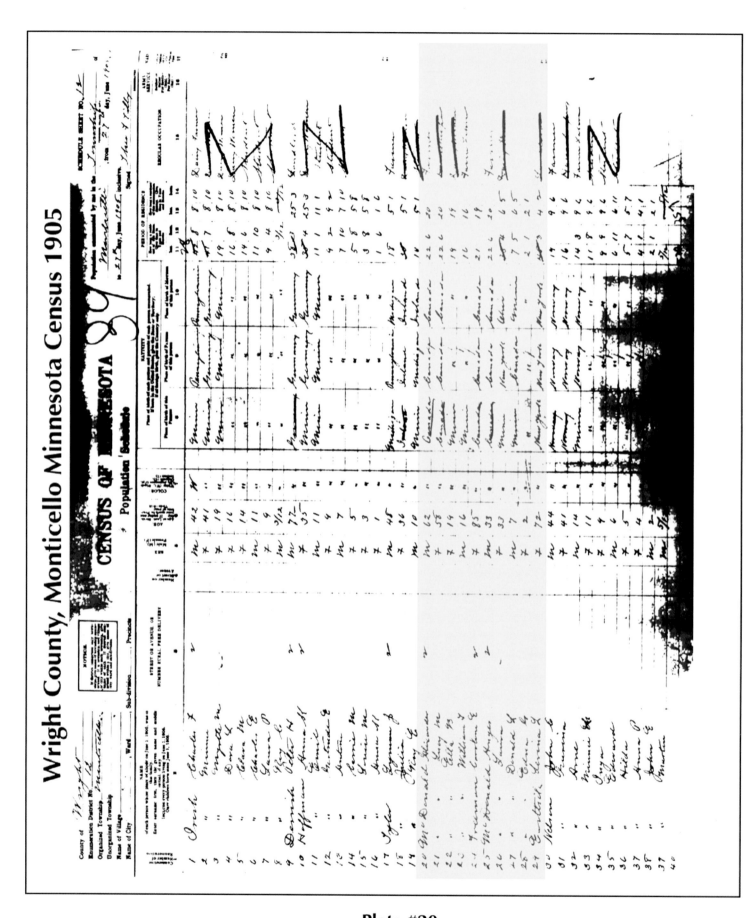

Plate #20

THE CHILDREN AND GRANDCHILDREN OF LAVINA DAY

Relationship by marriage

Children

JRI©2011

□ Persons born in Mankato

▨ Persons killed at Shetek

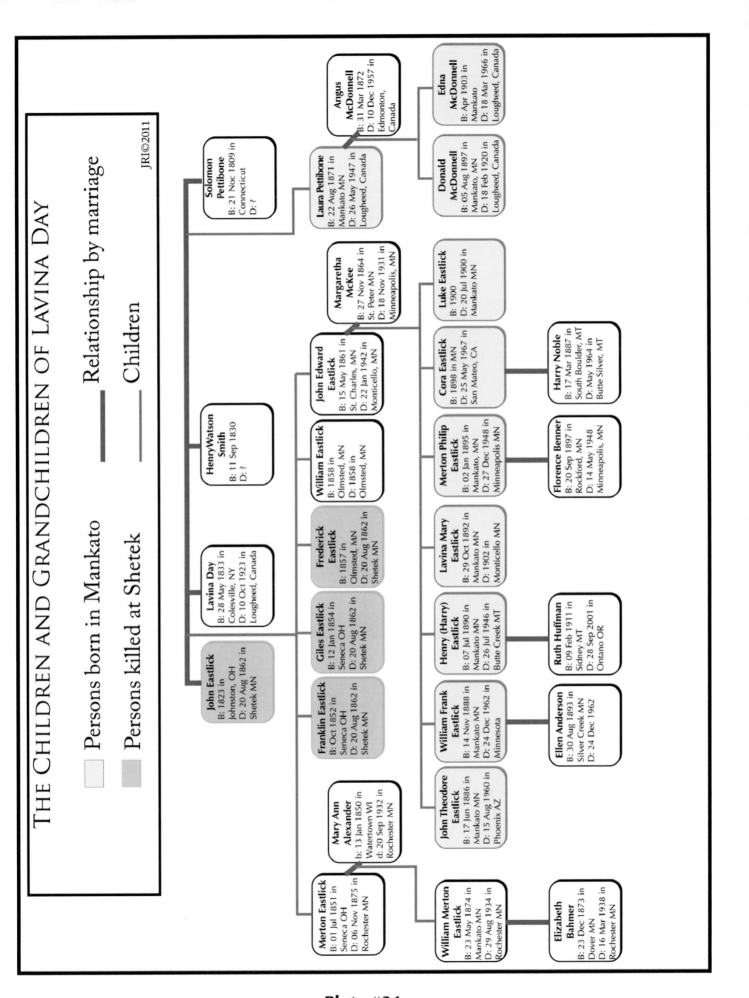

Plate #21

Lougheed, Canada

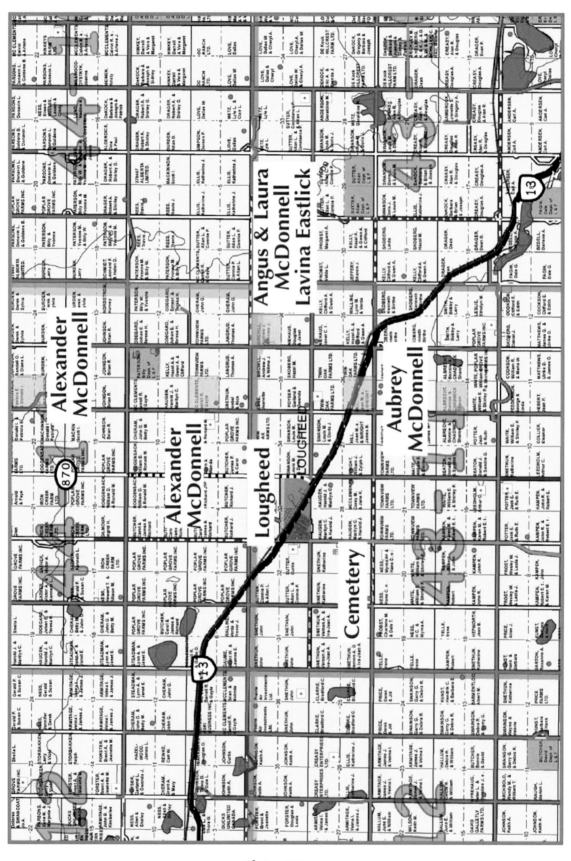

Plate #22

Lavina Eastlick's Travels

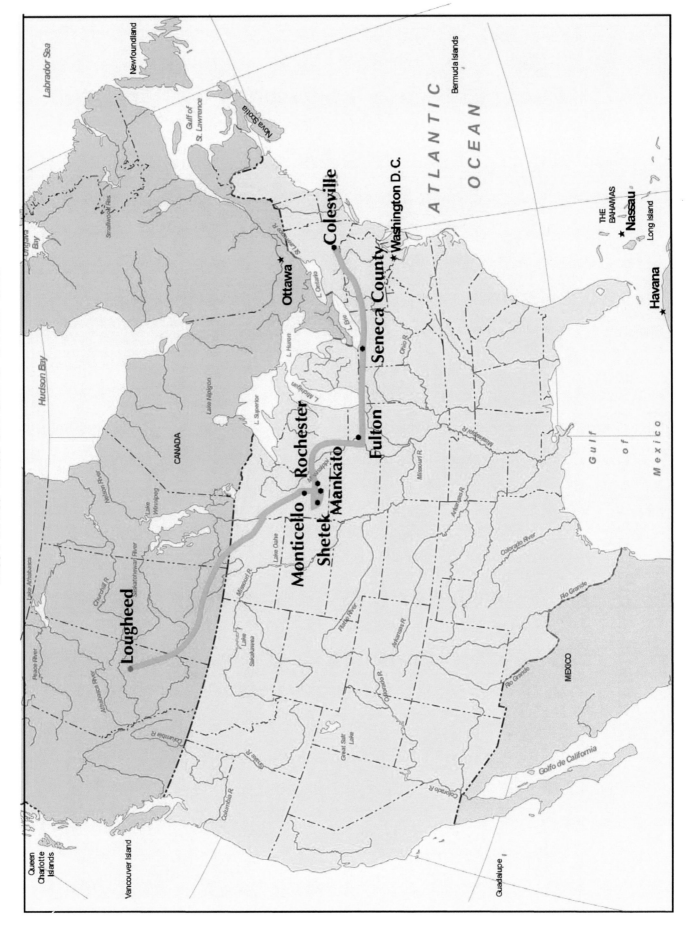

Plate #23

Andy Birchill Farmstead, Lougheed Alberta

Lower center, house with red roof: Andy Birchill, current owner's home. The white house just above was the home of Laura and Angus McDonnell where Lavina also lived until her death. Just north of the farmstead, in the wheat field, is a depression. To the left of that depression was the location of the sod house where Laura and Angus first lived when they came to Alberta. (Information from Andry Birchill.)

Plate #24